DRUMMING UP BUSINESS

Your Best Music Has Yet To Be Played

BOBBY DELVECCHIO

HigherLife Publishing & Marketing PO Box 623307
Oviedo, FL 32762 AhigherLife.com
Drumming Up Business – Robert DelVecchio – 1ˢᵗ ed.
ONE2BEAT Publishing
(407) 340-3663
www.DrummingUpBusiness.com

Cover design: Kelly Nielsen
Cover photo: Jon Maple
Library of Congress Control Number 1-9942806511
ISBN 978-1-951492-84-7 Hardback
ISBN 978-1-951492-85-4 Paperback
ISBN 978-1-951492-90-8 eBook

10 9 8 7 6 5 4 3 2 1

Printed in the United States of America.

THE BEAT ON THE STREET
Testimonials

"Bobby, you are the current day Renaissance Man."

—**Scott Griffiths,** Franchisor and the co-author of *Beyond Genius: The 12 Essential Traits of Today's Renaissance Man.*

"Bobby has lived a life as an all in, innovative sales professional, with a powerful message to share with the world."

—**Michael Crom** was the Chief Learning Officer at Dale Carnegie Training and co-author of *The Leader in You* and *The Sales Advantage.*

"Bobby's a world changer and a history maker. He'll speak to millions of people around the world. He is a valuable Gift of God (Ephesians 3:20)."

—**Pastor Paula White-Cain** is an American pastor, author, and televangelist. She is the Senior Pastor of New Destiny Christian Center, a non-denominational, multicultural megachurch.

"Bobby Del was one of the best drummers ever."

—**Arnie Silver** was one of the original members of the Dovells, an American doo-wop group with hit records "You Can't Sit Down" and "Bristol Stomp."

"Bob's talents became an important part of the show. When new legends (Chuck Berry, Jackie Wilson, Chubby Checker, and Bo Diddley) joined the show, they asked if Bobby Del was the drummer and, in some cases, wanted it in their contracts. This was an unheard-of request at that time."

—**Ray Reneri**, Manager, Dick Clark's Cavalcade/ Caravan of Stars and Rich Nader's Rock and Roll Revival. Tour Manager for Little Richard, Mitch Ryder & the Detroit Wheels, The Ronettes, The Shirelles, Tommy James & The Shondells, The Supremes, The Four Tops, The Temptations, Stevie Wonder, Tom Jones, Judy Garland, Herman's Hermits, The Rolling Stones, The Animals, The Who, The McCoys, Ricky Nelson, Elvis Presley, The Beatles, The Rolling Stones, Liza Minelli, Rosemary Clooney, Moscow on Ice, River Dance, The Duke Ellington Orchestra, Willie Nelson, David Cassidy, Don Rickles, Joan Rivers, Reba McIntyre, Kenny Rogers, The Four Seasons, Jay and the Americans, Tony Bennett, Frankie Avalon, The Yardbirds, Jeff Beck, Jimmy Page, and Eric Clapton. Ray helped organize The Beatles' Shea Stadium Show and was Stage Manager for Hurricane Sandy Relief concert "12-12-12" with The Rolling Stones, Paul McCartney, Eric Clapton, Bruce Springsteen, Billy Joel, and Alicia Keys.

"I consider Bob as my American son. He is one of the most entertaining speakers and creative storytellers that I've ever met."

—**Dr. NakaMats** is considered the #1 Inventor in the World with over 3,500 inventions including: The Floppy Disc, the computer, the CD and DVD, Cinemascope, Love Jet, etc. He has won the Grand Prix #1 prize at the Inventors Convention in NYC sixteen times.

"Bobby you have that 'Brilliant Spark' that I often talk about in my books."

—**Simon T. Bailey,** *Success Magazine's* 2018 Top 25, Hall of Fame speaker, and renowned teacher, the author of *Shift Your Brilliance: Harness the Power of You, Inc.* and *Release Your Brilliance.* He was inducted into the National Speakers Association CPAE Speaker Hall of Fame.

"Bob DelVecchio is the Battery King. He knows how to drive music and business."

—**Billy Osborne** was named *Metronome* magazine's Best New Drummer performing with the legends: Wes Montgomery, Archie Shepp, John Coltrane, and Friends of Distinction. In 1990, he was Ray Charles's right-hand man in writing, arranging and producing.

"Bobby, you are born to win. Drumming Up Business will unleash your symphony of success."

—**Tom Ziglar** is the proud son of Zig Ziglar and the CEO of Ziglar, Inc.

When I met Zig Ziglar:
"Bobby you're a salesman!"
"No, Zig, I'm a rock drummer!"
He explained, (drummer definition 2) a traveling salesman—one who "drums up business."

—**Zig Ziglar** achieved the Silver Buffalo Award from Boy Scouts of America, which is their highest award in the United States for services to youth. He launched his own company to offer training in sales, business, and personal development. Books include *See You at the Top, Confessions of a Happy Christian,* and *Secrets of Closing the Sale.*

"Put this on your calendar to buy and learn about the amazing journey of a man who has done more for humanity than most Nobel laureates!"

—**Nick Neonakis** is an author, the CEO of The Franchise MBA, and the CEO of The Franchise Consulting. He is the world leader in franchise sales with over 150 franchise consultants under his brokerage and helps individuals and businesses with their franchise acquisitions.

"Bobby is a dear friend whom I love. From the moment I met Bobby I felt the Holy Spirit working through him. As I began to hear his testimony I realized that I have met a humble man that has done amazing things in his life. These things were all done throughout a life of diversity and yet he always finds a way to be thankful. As we have become great friends, I count myself blessed to have him in my life. Bobby needs to keep on rocking, as God has truly made him special and a blessing to so many. God gifted him with drum sticks to reach those who are in need, and gave him a heart of gold, always giving credit to our Lord and Savior Jesus Christ. Oh, and he is also an amazing business man who can be trusted at every level."

—**Joe Bloncko**, CEO of Kingdom Impact Investments (KII), a company that was created to deploy private capital initiatives primarily in the real estate marketplace. KII and its principles have successfully created and developed some of the most desired capital investment structures and models known in the industry today. Utilizing these unique structures and models, KII aims to fund the development and successful completion of billions of dollars of investments.

"During your lifetime you might be lucky to meet one person who is a larger-than-life person, who has been part of music royalty and history, with the talent and skill of a businessman, a loving father, a loyal friend, a sharp dresser, who remains a 'class act' at all times. If you add that all together you get Bob Delvecchio.

"Bob, I am honored to call you my friend. You are a 'Gladiator' not a spectator!"

—**Johnny C. Ferraro**, Creator/Producer, American Gladiators

"When I think of Bob DelVecchio, I think of enthusiasm. He exudes it, in everything that he does. In the forty years that we have collaborated on many different projects, I have never met anyone who equals the energy Bob brings to accomplishing the goals he sets for his clients and for himself. His experience as a performer brings a unique perspective to his business clients."

—**Carl Zwisler**, Attorney, Lathrop GPM Chief. Staff Counsel/General Counsel, Director of Legal and Governmental Affairs, International Franchise Association. Author of *The Basics of Master Franchising*. Honors: The Best Lawyers in America©; The International Who's Who of Franchise Lawyers; Who's Who Legal Thought Leaders; Legal Eagles Hall of Fame, Franchise Times.

"Bob is an amazingly inspiring guy who knows how to motivate you to be your best. I would not be where I am today if it weren't for his guidance early on my career. I am proud to call him friend."

—**Aaron Pearce**, Grammy Award Winning and 30 time MultiPlatinum Producer/Songwriter for: Michael Jackson, Stevie Wonder, Justin Bieber, Jennifer Lopez, Brian McKnight, Ricky Martin, Pitbull, Celine Dion, New Kids on the Block, Mary J. Blige, John Legend, Boyz II Men, and American Idol.

"Bob is on fire for life and everything that he does is fueled with passion, heart and creativity. His expertise in franchising and music combined into one book is an explosive combination."

—**Edith Wiseman**, CFE President of FRANdata, has worked with more than 5,000 franchise brands and 9,000+ lenders through the Franchise Registry.

"Bobby, a truly Divine Appointment. So grateful to fight shoulder to shoulder with you! Love You, My Brother."

—**Mark Koch**, Author, *The First Hour for Men*, Speaker, and Hollywood Film Producer. He has produced several A-list films including *Black Dog* with Patrick Swayze, *The Perfect Game* with Cheech Marin, and the number one blockbuster hit, *Lost in Space*.

"Bobby's Faith and Legacy. Bobby's positive outlook on life is contagious. He has successfully franchised the MindChamps International Preschool to the USA.

Bobby always focuses on his blessings that he already has and not what he is missing in life. One of Bobby's passion is helping people build successful businesses that they can pass on to their children.

Bobby's unwavering faith in God and his commitment to his family have been the cornerstone of his life. Bobby remains grounded in his values and committed to making a difference in the world."

—**Ben Ang,** Chief Business Development Officer,
MindChamps International Preschool, USA

"Bobby's leadership skills over the years has allowed him to build a successful business and corporate team. His professionalism with his clients typically results in long lasting friendships. Bobby's dedication to his religion and family shows through his desire to grow every day. His great communication and rapid response to business ideas is unparalleled. Working with Bobby has been a great experience for our company as we continue learning from a proven expert in our field."

Trey Kessler
Chief Executive Officer, Grain and Berry

"God bless Bob Delvecchio. I admire his faith in God. I share his passion. This is the BEST BOOK I have read this year. It has impacted my life! He is a legendary entertainer. More importantly he is a legendary compassionate gentleman, always going the extra mile for everyone. I learned so many golden nuggets in his brilliant book. Can you say BEST SELLER?"

—**Bruce Merrin,** President, Bruce Merrin's
Celebrity Speakers & Entertainment

"We are more than a conquerors" (Rom. 8:37). "The LORD will make you the head not the tail" (Deut. 28:13). Keep me as the apple of your eye" (Psalm 17:8). "I can do everything through him who gives me strength" (Phil. 4:13). "We are heirs … of God and co-heirs of Christ" (Rom. 8:17). "He who unites himself with the LORD is one with him in spirit" (1Cor. 6:17 BSB). "For I know the plans I have for you … plans to prosper you and not to harm you, plans to give you hope and a future" (Jer. 29:11).

—GOD

It is with heartfelt feelings,
that this book is dedicated to:

Gina DelVecchio-Handy—Mom
Daira Traynor—Daughter
Sean DelVecchio—Son
Philip DelVecchio—Father
Gary DelVecchio—Brother
Sean Traynor—Son-in Law
Ellen DelVecchio—Daughter-in Law
Jane DelVecchio—Granddaughter

"I'll give you Panovision pictures,
'Cos you give me Technicolor dreams."
—Bee Gees

REPERTOIRE
Table of Contents

DRUM BREAK
Foreword

My name is Dr. NakaMats from Tokyo, Japan. I currently hold the record for inventions, according to the Guinness Book of World Records, with over 3,200 to my credit—three times that of my closest rival, Thomas Edison. My inventions include the computer, floppy disk, the CD, the DVD, the digital watch, Cinemascope, the synthesizer, karaoke, and the taxicab meter.

I have known and worked with Bob DelVecchio for the past thirty years. As my Ambassador to the U.S., he has helped promote me through many appearances on national TV shows, colleges, and professional organizations. For years he has successfully represented many of my products through distribution in the U.S.

He has emceed for me for several of my seminars and I am proud to be associated with him. He is one of the most entertaining speakers that I've met. He has a great respect and understanding of my nature and ways of conducting business. I consider Bob my "American Son." I know as my protégé he has learned several valuable lessons from me and he applies them very well in his life and in his business.

It has been a pleasure working with Bob. He is one of the best sales and marketing people that I've ever known. He has a creative but practical approach to business practices. He has a very positive and outgoing personality. He once asked me what the definition of success was, and I said, "one word … Persistence." One of the greatest characteristics that he possesses is his persistence—he has a "Never Surrender" attitude. That is what I believe true Champions are made from.

I believe that Bob and I will have a life-long relationship, and I look forward to many more successful ventures with him.

Sincerely,

SIR Dr. NakaMats

THE SHOW MUST GO ON
Introduction

Welcome Back My Friends To the Show that Never Ends!

"The show must go on" is a phrase in show business, meaning that regardless of what happens, whatever show has been planned still has to be staged for the waiting patrons.

One stormy winter day, as I was coming back from The Magnificent Yankees Drum Corp Practice, the car I was riding in got sideswiped and slid off the road. It tumbled and rolled ten times until the top was smashed in. I was pulled out of the upside-down car with a broken clavicle and lay in the snow for an hour before an ambulance arrived to take me to the hospital, where my fractured shoulder was reset.

That evening, I had to play a concert with my rock band in front of thousands of people. With my left arm in a sling, I played the whole concert with my right arm and didn't miss a beat, because … "the show must go on."

You see, even in the most unfavorable, drastic and unfortunate situations, you need to draw upon your inner strength to persevere and succeed.

Let me tell you a little story of how and when I knew I wanted to be a public speaker. In my twelfth grade impromptu speech class, the teacher would put various topics on pieces of paper in a box, and we would draw a topic and discuss it for five minutes. One day, the first student drew the word "wall" and gave a dissertation on what a wall meant to him. He talked about the many kinds of walls, such as the Great Wall of China and the Berlin Wall, how walls separate rooms, the walls we construct in our minds, and so on.

Then it was my turn. I drew a topic, stared at it, and shared what it meant to me. I must point out that my vision is not perfect and I was too vain to wear glasses. I proceeded to talk about genital herpes, HPV, syphilis, gonorrhea, and crabs. The whole class burst out in laughter, not about the topic, but the fact I had picked something about sex. I looked over at the teacher, who was beet red with anger and said, "Mr. DelVecchio, that's not funny. The topic was Veterans Day, not venereal disease." The class was now in hysterics—at that point I realized I wanted to be a public speaker.

Against All Odds

At one and a half years old, my parents noticed that I had a hard time standing and walking. They took me to nine different doctors who could not give a diagnosis. The tenth doctor unveiled the devastating news, "I'm sorry, but your son has polio." He told them that in the best-case scenario, I would be a cripple for the rest of my life. In the worst case, I would only live about six months.

But that was not God's verdict. My mom proceeded to massage my affected right leg with rubbing alcohol and gave me extremely hot baths to ease the pain. My dad went out and bought two bass drums, so that I could strengthen my legs with enjoyable exercise. I "beat" polio with no serious aftereffects. I have since become an advocate for polio eradication treatment, regularly speaking for the Rotary Club International.

What Satan meant for evil against me, God used for good. I guess you can say, I was born to be a drummer.

Noted motivational speaker Zig Ziglar said, when he met me for the first time, "So, Bobby, you're a salesman."

"No, Zig, I'm a drummer."

"Like I said, Bobby, you're a salesman."

"Zig, with all due respect, I couldn't sell anybody anything," I said. "I'm a rock-and-roll drummer."

Then Zig asked me, "Do you know the definition of a drummer?"

"Sure," I said, "a person who beats a drum."

"Yes, that's the first definition," he said. "The second is a traveling salesman. That's where the saying 'drumming up business' comes from. In the past, the drummer was a salesman. He would bang his drum to announce his presence, and people would come out to buy his goods. Like I said, Bobby, you are a salesman."

Indeed, I am both a drummer and a salesman. I have been a drummer for many well-known bands for decades. And in the past thirty-five years, I have sold three thousand franchises in eighty countries. I represent more than three hundred franchisors and have a proven track record of finding people who have the resources and business prowess to become successful franchisees. I believe the key to successful franchising is *building relationships with people and companies*. You drum up business by building relationships.

Everything I Am Today, I Owe to Rock & Roll

I am at that pinnacle point in my life where experience meets wisdom. This is the perfect time for me to share important life and business lessons with other people. Someone once told me, "Bob, you are a conductor." Those in the orchestra are your protégés, and the lights and focus are on them. When the orchestra plays its show-stopping performance and the audience gives a standing ovation, you turn around and take a bow. In the finale, it's all about the audience. In other words, the one you serve is the most important judge.

This book chronicles my experience, but now the spotlight is on you. You have the opportunity to take the lessons I've learned from my personal and professional life and make them work for you in a positive way.

One day while I was praying, I asked God, "What's in store for the second half of my life? I've been so blessed in my first half."

Sometimes, God talks in riddles. He told me, "Use your experience to help others. Put everything you've done in your life together, and that's what you'll do."

So, I took an inventory of my life. *Let's see, I've been a drummer; I played with major bands, had hit records; and I've started companies, sold franchises, and opened businesses. I've been … drumming up business. WOW!*

I'm going to be helping people drum up more business and become successful at whatever they do in life. You could say this book was God-ordained.

I have survived polio, cancer, divorce, and a lot of other hurdles in life. God used them to make me stronger. We all face obstacles and setbacks. The key is to learn what they are intended to teach us. I have a genuine desire to impart my wisdom to you so that you can learn from my mistakes and victories. I want you to be the *"One 2 Beat"*!

It sounds easy enough—deciding what you want and then acting as if you have it already. So why don't people do it? Fear is one main reason. Fear is the enemy. Take these steps to defeat fear:

1. Step out of your fear. Fear blocks your success. Choose to not surrender to it.

2. Do the things you fear the most.

3. Your thoughts are the things that define your life, so don't think about your fear. Focus on the one who can cast out fear—Jesus

4. Watch what comes out of your mouth. If you say it, you own it.

5. Act as if you are not afraid. Live by faith.

6. Redefine your fears as challenges and exciting opportunities, not problems. When you overcome poverty of the mind or the scarcity mentality, success and achievement come easily.

7. The mind can hold only one thought at a time: positive or negative. Your choice! Make it positive!

8. Successful people think and talk about what they want. Unsuccessful people talk about what they don't want!

9. Belief is the power of the made-up mind.

10. First, decide what you want, then totally dedicate yourself to achieve it.

11. Act as if you already have it. Winners take responsibility. They offer no excuses.

12. Decide what you want; think in terms of having it now.

13. Act successful, happy, enthusiastic and confident.

14. Act as though your goals have been met. What the mind can conceive, it can achieve.

My phrase, be the "One 2 Beat," comes from a childhood memory of mine. When I was growing up in Rome, New York, some kids and I used to play a game called King of the Mountain. We were all five to seven years old. We had gotten a lot of snow, and there was a mountain of snow that we called "Mount Everest." It had to be at least four to five feet tall. Or maybe it just seemed that way to us because we were small.

The kid who was on the top of that pile was the King of the Mountain, and we had to knock him off the mountain. So, the guy at the top, was he the best? No. Was he number one? No. But he was the "One 2

Beat." I remind people all the time that they don't have to be the best; they just have to be the "One 2 Beat."

One day, somebody asked me, "Bobby, are you the best drummer?"

I said, "I don't know if I'm the best drummer. I'm a very good drummer."

"Well, are you … number one?"

I said, "I can't answer that because nobody is the number one drummer. Are you talking about jazz, country, rock, heavy metal?"

There are great drummers in all those types of music. But I'll tell you this: I'm the "One 2 Beat." I strongly believe that to be successful in any aspect of life, you need to strive to be the "One 2 Beat." *Drumming Up Business* is the story of my journey through my life and career over the past fifty-five years, told through the language of music.

It's for those who want to increase their business production, have more personal joy, and reach their full potential in life. It will help crystallize your purpose in life (with a plan) so that your legacy will live on forever.

> *Every day that you talk and act is telling the world who you are.*
> **Bobby DelVecchio**

Today, most developing countries are crying out for the kind of expertise you possess. But this is big league stuff, so only those who possess courage, vision, know-how, and determination need apply. You, as a business or professional person, have the leverage to influence the world.

> *Stop whining, they only tackle the man with the ball.*
> **Bobby DelVecchio**

My goal for this book is to *encourage* you to live up to your full potential, *equip* you with the tools you need to succeed, and *elevate* your sense of purpose and direction in life so that you become the "One 2 Beat"!

Are you committed to living your dreams? Let's get started.

> **"I was born to do something no one's ever done, no one's ever done before!"**

THE GOOD FOOT
Positive Attitude

"Attitude makes altitude."

—Zig Ziglar

A few years ago, I was feeling some discomfort in my throat, so I went to my doctor. He told me, "Don't worry about it; it's probably only swollen glands."

That didn't sound right, so I went to an ear, nose, and throat specialist who told me, "You have throat cancer. We will do a biopsy to confirm it." The result … stage four throat cancer. Give me a break! How shocking is that? I was taken aback by the news, but I didn't cry. In fact, I wasn't even discouraged. My friends asked me, "Bobby, when you found out you had cancer, did your life flash before your eyes?"

I replied, "Yes, it did, and it was amazing."

If the doctor had told me, "You have cancer, and it's terminal," I would have told him, "Your report might say it's terminal, but God's report says I am not just a contender; I am a conqueror in Jesus Christ. I didn't survive cancer—I *beat* it. So, get on the 'good foot.'" A positive attitude makes altitude.

Get on the "Good Foot"

My mom would say to me, "Put your best foot forward," and I had a boss who would say, "Make a powerful first impression." But James Brown said it best: You "got to get on the good foot." We need to do this from the time we get up in the morning and while completing our activities at home and work throughout the day. It's all about having a positive attitude.

This chapter is the most important one in the book because, to me, a positive attitude is the most important aspect of life and business. How can you drum up business with a negative attitude? How can you have a happy marriage or happy friendship with a negative attitude? We need to remain positive every day, in every situation, whether it relates to our health, our relationships, or our bank accounts.

You "got to get on the good foot."

Surround Yourself with Positive People

After driving all night with my band of musicians, we arrived in the Big Apple at four a.m. Not having a big budget, we decided to sleep in the car and equipment trailer to save money. We drove across the George Washington Bridge to New Jersey and pulled off the side of the road to get some rest. The next morning, we were suddenly awakened by the loud whistle of a train approaching. We jumped out of the car thinking we had parked on the tracks. Well, we weren't parked on the tracks, but we had pulled off next to the city dump. We now reeked of odor and thirst. We found a hotel to wash up in and put on clean clothes. As we left the hotel, arm in arm, we broke out in a song:

Oh, we ain't got a barrel of money
Maybe we're ragged and funny
But we'll travel along,
Singing a song,
Side by side.

Adversity Brings Out the Best in Some and the Worst in Others

Avoid the bad foot—you gotta do it on the good foot. A negative attitude will never get you anywhere. It takes more energy to frown than to smile. One way to keep a negative attitude from consuming you is to be careful about the company you keep. Surround yourself with positive people. Don't be S.N.I.O.P. (Susceptible to the Negative Influence of Other People).

Being influenced by others can happen in many ways, even subconsciously. Those who influence you might not realize it themselves. Overall, the people around us affect us and help shape our character. The people who inspire you shape your life. They help give context to what you're passionate about. As I grew up watching those around me work toward their goals and make crucial decisions, I was inspired and influenced to launch my own companies.

There's no denying certain relationships are more challenging than others, but through each one, we have an opportunity to grow and help others do the same. Every relationship teaches us something about loving, trusting, forgiving, setting boundaries, taking care of ourselves, and taking care of each other. From the people who love you to the people who challenge you, to the people who support you in life, it's important to show your gratitude. As we grow older, we change, either for the better or, unfortunately, for the worse. In either case, people around us play a huge factor in directing changes in our character. One person can make a huge difference in your life, whereas ten people all together might never change you.

It would be quite hard to live in today's culture without being influenced by someone or some type of experience. Life is full of influences, some positive and some negative. The way you react to an influence determines what kind of impact you will receive from the influence.

Whenever anyone was arguing in our house, my Aunt Josephine LaMonica (we called her Jo Jo) would say, "It's all right, it's okay, I'll make a pizza!" And everybody stopped arguing. It worked like magic!

When your well-being depends on having satisfied customers, even one complaint can set you on a downward spiral by darkening your perspective and mindset. With this attitude controlling you, complaints will increase, and pessimism will define more of your character. Each negative comment and thought moves you down the slippery slope. The lower you go, the faster you slide. Once it was said of a person, "He had a photographic mind, but only turned out negatives." Don't be that person.

It is still possible to apply the brakes on negative thinking. It takes a conscious effort to counteract negativity with positivity. When something bad happens, do what you can to improve the situation, learn the lesson from it, tell yourself and your team members it will get better, and move on.

Joy is not dependent on your circumstances. Some of the world's most miserable people live in what many would consider the best circumstances. People who reach the top of the ladder of success are often surprised to find emptiness awaiting them.

Striving for perfection is a losing game. If your goal is to be perfect, what happens when you achieve perfection, if that's even possible? It's the imperfection that keeps motivating us to push further and harder. Look for, and focus on, the positive spin on every negative situation.

Derive Strength from God

We cannot sustain a positive attitude using just our human effort. We need God's strength to stay positive in the face of all the negativity in the world.

Hire People with a Positive Attitude

Having been in the franchise business for more than thirty-five years, I have interviewed many people for sales and administrative positions. People are on their best behavior during an interview, so how do you know which candidate is your best pick? Like everything else in life, it all boils down to attitude.

So, I use a code to assess candidates. The code has two digits. One is my assessment of the candidate's attitude, and the second digit scores the candidate's apparent ability. A score of one is the best, two is okay, and three is no way. For example, if a candidate is a one-two, meaning that he is the best in terms of attitude and okay in terms of ability, I will hire him. I will never hire anyone who scores a three on attitude. Woody Hayes, the famed football coach at Ohio State said, "You win with people." He knew the player who played from his heart could overcome what he lacked in ability.

> We need God's strength to stay positive in the face of all the negativity

You've probably heard the expression, "You can lead a horse to water, but you can't make him drink." Yes, you can—you've just gotta find out what makes him thirsty! Counteract negativity with positivity.

"Positive thinking will let you do everything better than negative thinking will."
—**Zig Ziglar**

One summer, I felt like I really needed a trip to the ocean. So I went to the beach, but the ocean seemed to say, "It's not in me!" The ocean did not do for me what I thought it would. Then I said, "Perhaps the mountains will provide the rest I need." So, I went to the mountains. When I woke the first morning, I gazed at the magnificent mountain I had so longed to see. But the sight did not satisfy me. The mountain said, "It's not in me!"

What I really needed was the vast ocean of God's love, in the high mountain of His truth within me. His wisdom provides more comfort and strength than the ocean or mountains could ever provide. His wisdom far surpasses the value of jewels, gold, or precious stones. Christ *is* wisdom, and He fills our deepest needs. Our inner restlessness can be pacified only by His eternal friendship and love for us.

"The winner's edge is not in a gifted birth, a high IQ, or in talent. The winner's edge is all in the ATTITUDE, not aptitude."
—**Denis Waitley**

Know Your Worth

Feeling inferior or worthless is something that troubles many people day in and day out. It's hard to be on the "good foot" when you're feeling inferior to others. When I tell people that the way they feel is a choice and that they can change it in an instant, they don't think that's possible. Why do they say that? Because they have been conditioned their entire lives to think they are worth nothing. Maybe they were beaten or abused when they were children. Maybe they were raised with some form of addiction in the household. Whatever the heck it is, it's holding them back. It's holding them prisoner and keeping them from achieving their full potential in life.

Around the turn of the century, a bar of steel was worth about five dollars. Yet when forged into horseshoes, it was worth $10; when made into needles, it's value was $350; when used to make small pocketknife blades, it was worth $32,000; when made into the springs for watches, it's value increased to $250,000. What a pounding the steel bar had to endure to be worth this much! But the more it was shaped, hammered, put through fire, beaten, and polished, the greater its value. May we use this analogy as a reminder to be still, silent, long-suffering, for it is those who suffer the most who yield the most (Lang 2018).

You are worth more than you know. If I wrote you a check right now for one million dollars to remove your fingers or your arms, would you do it? *Of course not!* We haven't even gotten to the good parts yet, and you already know you're worth more than a million dollars.

Even if you had all the money in the world, what use would it be if you couldn't enjoy being able to do the things you love to do, with full mobility? It would be worthless to you. It wouldn't be worth anything! When you recognize that no amount of money is as valuable as your unique talents, freedom, health, and loved ones, you are subconsciously telling yourself, "I am worth everything!" You have just taken the first step in rewiring your brain to think with a prosperity and abundance-based mindset.

This type of exercise can ultimately empower you to create *anything* you want in life. You can have *anything*, my friend—truly. Focus on what you do have, and let positive thoughts propel you through every day with hope and enthusiasm. When you have negative thoughts, immediately eradicate them from your mind and your life. The more you do this, the more you will have *only* positive thoughts.

The mind, or in this case the ego, is so scared of the unknown, the emptiness, and the silence between and around every living and nonliving thing that it has to create a false identity that allows it to control your thoughts and actions. A self-centered ego is detrimental to your overall health because it takes *way* more energy to act in a negative way than it does to act in a positive way. Now, here is where it gets *really* powerful. The very moment you realize that the ego has no true power over you and that it cannot control you in any way, shape, or form, it instantly goes away. It disappears.

Every time a negative thought or emotion comes into your head, I want you to acknowledge its presence in your mind and simply ask yourself, "Why am I thinking or feeling that right now?" Then understand that those types of thoughts are always controlled by your ego, while your committed nature emits nothing but pure love and positivity. This best is done by having a positive relationship with Jesus Christ.

At that point, your ego no longer has any power over you. You have now brought your *true self* to the forefront and are ready to live in a new way. If this sounds crazy to you, then do yourself the biggest favor in the world and just give it a shot. Seriously, test it out.

Decide What You Want, and Claim It

Success means different things to different people. Here are some of my thoughts about success. They all relate to having a positive attitude.

1. You are successful when you have a definite, worthwhile, written goal with a precise date, and you are moving toward it.

2. Achievement has nothing to do with talent or opportunities; it is a result of conditioning and planning.

3. People face mediocrity and failure because of *poverty of the mind*, which comes from negative thinking.

The Ego Has Landed

So, I was on this flight from Dallas to New York, in first class, and the flight attendant asked me, "Mr. Delvecchio, would you like the salmon or the chicken Caesar salad for lunch?"

I said, "I think I'll have the salmon today. "

The guy next to me said, "You're not Bobby DelVecchio, are you?"

And I said, "Yes, I am. Why?"

He said, "I am your biggest fan."

Thinking he was remembering me as a rock drummer for some of the biggest bands, I said, "Thank you."

He said, "Can I have your autograph on this napkin?"

I said, "Sure," and signed my name.

I hadn't signed an autograph in some time. Then the lady behind me said, "No, I'm your biggest fan."

But by the time I finished, I had signed my name for everyone in first class. I was feeling very humbled but amazed at the same time that everyone knew me. As the plane landed, I got up and the man who was sitting next to me stood behind me and slapped me on the back and said, "There were some great rodeo champions, but you are the best one of them all."

Bobby DelVecchio was the world rodeo champion from Dallas Texas. In an Elvis impersonation voice, I said, "Thank you, thank you very much."

You might not think that having a big ego would cause a person to have a negative attitude. But the human ego can be an incredible negative influence on our mindset if we don't control it. Ego is definitely healthy and necessary, but it must be kept under control.

You can release your infinite potential and achieve anything you want to in life more easily than you could possibly imagine. There is only one problem: your mind is holding you back from everything you try to do in life because it is trying to create an identity for itself. This identity is what we call the "ego."

Having a positive attitude allows you to "get on the good foot." According to the Urban Dictionary, to "get on the good foot" is a Southernism that means "to begin a task, pronto. To get moving, get crackin', go forward—get your ass in gear."

When we "get on the good foot," it means we are happy, in a good mood.

In drumming, a "good foot" means the drummer has mastered his bass drum kick pedal, as well as independence, speed, style, and rhythm. When you get on the "good foot," you become independent and quick with style while you "tap" into the rhythm of life. Similarly, to "get in the groove" means to enter the spirit of the situation or circumstance of the moment. In musical terms, the "groove" is the track on an LP record that the needle of the record player had to ride in to reproduce the music.

Win with Enthusiasm

With a positive attitude comes enthusiasm, which is contagious. Being enthusiastic and optimistic makes your prospects and clients feel good

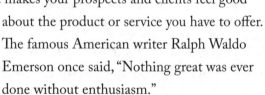

about the product or service you have to offer. The famous American writer Ralph Waldo Emerson once said, "Nothing great was ever done without enthusiasm."

"Nothing great was ever done without enthusiasm."

In one of my first presentations, I was just learning to sell, and a customer asked me, "What about this?"

I replied, "I don't know, but I know it's fantastic." Then he asked, "What about that?"

I said, "I'm not sure, but it's incredible."

The customer said, "You know what? You don't know anything, but you're so enthusiastic and excited that you got me excited. So, I'm going to buy it, and I don't even know why."

I asked Zig Ziglar once, "Will enthusiasm get every sale?"

He replied, "No, but it will get you more sales than if you didn't have it."

One way to act as though you already have what you want is through visualization—imagining and visualizing the things you want:

1. Garbage in, garbage out. Think good thoughts.

2. Change your programming by changing your input.

3. Visualize success, and see yourself already succeeding.

4. Your vision of who you are is who you are.

Another way to make your success manifest and to dissolve your fear is by repeating affirmations, or positive statements you tell yourself:

1. Reprogram your mind with your visions and affirmations.

2. Affirmations must always be in the present tense, such as, "I am competent and successful."

3. Your mind doesn't know the difference between what is real and what is imagined. So, imagine success and abundance without limits.

4. Imagine your life as you wish it to be.

5. Write down five affirmations, and read them every day.

Uncle Teddy: "Because, Maxwell, what you do defines who you are!"

Maxwell: "No, Uncle Teddy, who you are defines what you do!"

—Across the Universe (2007 Movie)

Let the Past Go

You're only as good as your last hit record—at least that's the way it seems, given society's obsession with success. Recently, on a late-night TV program, I saw a teenage idol who lost everything to alcohol and a string of failed marriages attempting to resurrect the glory of his career. As he labored through forgotten ballads in a voice long in need of retirement, I felt sad for him.

None of us can live on the glory of our past successes. Like it or not, yesterday's home runs don't win today's baseball games. Most of us have received a few awards along the way, and we experience the thrill of momentary applause and recognition. But as time passes, memories fade, and people change. Life goes on. Those diminishing accolades are no more than perishable wealth. They often come at great personal prices. And when the stage lights fade on your notoriety, what do you do? When you are no longer in control, how do you react? Get angry? Start throwing things? Have a pity party? Blame others?

> *We are hard pressed on every side, but not crushed; perplexed, but not in despair; persecuted, but not abandoned; struck down, but not destroyed.*
> **—2 Corinthians 4:8–9**

Looking back fondly on past achievements and accolades is not productive. Instead, look to the future. Get on the "good foot." Make some new memories. Achieve accomplishments so amazing that they blow the old ones away. As the old saying goes, "Let go and let God." Your best music has yet to be played.

The ultimate freedom is the ability to embrace the right attitude.

Keep in mind that the ultimate freedom is the ability to embrace the right attitude. Your attitude is the captain of your will. It will determine what actions you will take. You can choose to be still and know that God is in control, or you can choose to selfishly wrestle back that control. Self-pity is a common reaction when people don't have control over a situation and don't get their way. Be careful with this; self-pity will nurture a "victim mentality." We must take responsibility for our own shortcomings in life instead of blaming others. Avoid saying or thinking statements like, "No one appreciates me," "No one understands me," "I had a rough childhood," or "They took advantage of me." And remember Rodney Dangerfield's classic line, "I don't get no respect"? None of that matters! We must remember that we will face trials as humans, but God is bigger than any problem we face. This gives us ample reason to be positive.

JIM CARREY'S RULES FOR SUCCESS

Top 10 Drum Tips—How to Become the "One 2 Beat"

1. Visualize Your Success

2. See Challenges as Beneficial

3. Follow Your Passion

4. Be a Creator

5. Risk Being Yourself

6. Compromise

7. Don't Let Fear Hold You Back

8. Believe

9. Have Intuition

10. Take a Chance

Before we move on to Beat 4, let's review the strategies covered in this chapter:

1. Put your "good foot"—your positive attitude—forward.

2. Win with enthusiasm.

3. Surround yourself with positive people.

4. Hire people with a positive attitude.

5. Counteract negativity with positivity.

6. Derive strength from God.

7. Know your worth.

8. Realize that "the ego has landed." Control your ego.

9. Decide what you want, and claim it.

10. Let the past go.

HEART BEAT
Passion. Dreams.

Remember back when you were a kid? ... You had BIG dreams!

You wanted to climb Mt. Everest and scuba dive to the depths of the ocean. You wanted to be a ballerina on Broadway or the bravest fireman on Earth. There was nothing that could stop you. You were invincible! And then you grew up.

All those dreams vanished into the dark of night. Adulthood showed you the folly of dreaming big. You grew up, "matured," and left those "silly" dreams behind. Sound familiar? I challenge you to pull them out again. Dig deep and find those dreams you had ages ago and reevaluate them. Are they still what you want to do? Or has your dream changed? You do have dreams—and you CAN live them.

What Your Passion or Purpose Is in Life

One day at the airport as my family was going on vacation, I told my kids they could go to the newsstand and get some magazines to read on our trip. My son got *Popular Science* and *Popular Mechanics* (he was only four years old at the time). He was just learning to read, so I asked him why he got those magazines, and he said, "I find them really interesting." My daughter got *Billboard Music* magazine and *Seventeen* Magazine (she was eight years old at that time). Fast forward twenty years, my son is an engineer at Lockheed, and my daughter is a musician and owns a fashion company.

It doesn't matter what those dreams are. They may be travel-related, or they may be something else. What's important is that you pursue your passion and live your dream—wherever it may take you. You may feel overwhelmed by the bigness of it.

Your dream is HUGE, and perhaps you don't know how to do it. I know a thing or two about tackling big things. Here's how to do it. It really isn't that hard.

1. Remember that big things don't happen overnight.

Sir Edmund Hilary didn't climb Mt. Everest in a day. Neil Armstrong didn't wake up one morning and decide he'd fly to the moon. Steve Jobs didn't turn Apple into a multibillion-dollar empire overnight. Living your dream means taking a million (or more) teeny, tiny steps in the right direction. Many times, you won't even know which direction they're leading, but if you make sure you're doing what makes you happy, then your little steps are going the right way.

2. Remember that you won't achieve your dream in one fell swoop. If your dream is big enough, you'll get there step by step.

You won't achieve your dream in one fell swoop. You set your sights on the next manageable goal, and when you achieve that, you set another manageable goal. Mark Beaumont, world record holder as the fastest cyclist to circumnavigate the world, says, "If I focus on today, the big picture will take care of itself."

3. You won't learn everything you need to know immediately.

Don't expect to know everything you need to know right out of the gate. Your knowledge base will grow with each new experience you manage to successfully navigate. Give yourself time to slowly build up the bag of tricks you'll need to achieve your dream.

4. If you want to reach your unreachable star, you'll have to persevere. Big time.

There will be times when it's tough going, and you'll question whether or not you can succeed. There'll be times when it seems fruitless, and there's absolutely no progress whatsoever. That's when you take a deep breath, dig down deep, and persevere.

5. If I have only one suggestion for living your dream, it's to DO IT NOW!

Over-planning is the surest way to kill the dream. You need to plan enough so you don't kill yourself, but that's it. Don't try to plan out the tiniest detail and contemplate every contingency. If you do that, you'll soon be overwhelmed by the magnitude of what you're doing. It is possible to dream the impossible dream and reach the unreachable star—we're living proof of that. You can pursue your passion and live your dream. It's all up to you.

My mom once asked me what I was going to do when I grew up. I said, "I'm going to play at Madison Square Garden."

She asked me, "Do you know what Madison Square Garden is?"

"No," I said, "but I saw the Harlem Globetrotters basketball team on TV, and they were playing there. It really looked big. I want to play there sometime in a band."

I *have* played at Madison Square Garden more than a dozen times.

The big buzzword a few years back was, "Think outside the box." Then Deepak Chopra, the author and prominent figure in the New Age movement, said, "Get rid of the box."

Then I came along and said, "What box?" Let your passion and dreams be so spectacular that there is no room for them in a box. Don't confine yourself to the boxes other people might try to impose on you. Dream big, and let your passion carry you to new heights of success.

Dream B.I.G. (Believe In God)
—Bobby DelVecchio

Since your work is going to fill a large part of your life, the only way to be truly satisfied is to do what you believe is great work, and the only way to do great work is to love what you do. If you haven't found what you love yet, what you are passionate about, keep looking. Don't settle. Expose yourself to a lot of different life experiences. Listen to your inner heart— and to God's guidance— and follow your passion. Your passion is what will lead you to manifest your dreams.

God equips each of us with unique skills, strengths, and talents. Do not neglect the God-given gifts within you. Don't be careless with them, disregard them, or make light of them. Instead, meditate on them and apply them to your life. Don't dance around the issues related to becoming the "One 2 Beat." Jump into the water. Get committed! Multiple Dove Award Christian winner, Steven Curtis Chapman, sums it up:

> **Do not neglect the God-given gifts within you.**

"I'm diving in, I'm going deep."

Make sure what you are pursuing in life comes from who you are and what you believe. What you lack in experience, you can make up with the passion of your heart. What do you really, really want out of life? What excites you? What energizes you? What makes your heart beat faster? Nothing takes the place of passion. Passion is more valuable than intellect, talent, experience, enthusiasm, knowledge, rationality, and emotion. Passion and persistence are the keys to success and happiness.

"You make your own destiny; you have to do the best with what God gave you."
—**Forrest Gump's mom**

Channel Your Passion through Vision

"The only thing worse than being blind is having sight but no vision."
—**Helen Keller**

Once you have discovered your true passion in life, take some time to think about how to build your future around that passion. Create the vision that will lead you on a path to the greatest possible success in that endeavor. Where does your vision come from? The main source is the higher voice (God's). Don't let your vision be confined by your own limited capabilities. Only God knows what you are capable of. Look beyond yourself, even beyond your own lifetime, as you define your vision. If you rely only on your own perspective, you will miss the true potential of your life. To discover God's vision for your life, pray, read His Word, and look for signs. Where does God seem to be leading you?

Vision creates reality. We always have a vision of something before it actually becomes real to us. Sometimes we are faced with obstacles and temptations, and we are inclined to say that there is no point in even trying to continue. Instead of vision becoming real to us, we have entered a valley of defeat and pessimism. God gives us a vision, and then takes us into the valley to mold us into the shape of that vision. It is in the valley that so many of us give up and faint. Every God-given vision will become real if we will only have patience. While still in the light of the glory of the vision, we go out to achieve it, but the vision is not yet real to us. God has to take us into the valley and put us through fires and floods to shape us until we get to the point where He can trust us with the reality of the vision.

The vision you have today won't necessarily be the same vision you have ten years from now. As you go through different life stages, your priorities change. For example, when a young person graduates from college, his vision might be to rise through the ranks on Wall Street. He devotes all his time and effort into his career. Then, he falls in love, gets married, and has children, his vision will change. Working twelve-hour days in the heart of New York City is no longer where his passion lies, so he moves to a quieter, safer neighborhood in the suburbs and spends more time at home with his family.

At the corporate level, a management team might need to alter the company's vision based on a number of external influences. Maybe competition has escalated in their field, or maybe new technologies or consumer habits have altered the demand for their product or service. When the business climate changes, it's important to change direction as needed to maintain your competitive edge.

"A leader is a dealer in hope."

—Confucius

Lead through Vision

As a leader in your company, community, and family, others look to you for direction and inspiration. It is important that you define your group's vision and then share it in a compelling, consistent way. Even the most talented people around you can suffer from stagnation and a loss of interest, for whatever reason. They will look to you to restore their faith in the future. They will look to you for inspiration and bold confidence to accomplish great things. They will look to you for hope when economic and other conditions seem bleak.

Hope enables you to see, through the eyes of your heart, things that have not materialized yet. Make it a habit to hope for things you do not see yet in this life. Eagerly wait for the best outcome, and persevere through the difficult times.

> *"If I were to wish for anything, I should not wish for wealth and power, but for the passionate sense of the potential, for the eye which, ever young and ardent, sees the possible. Pleasure disappoints, possibility never. And what wine is so sparkling, what so fragrant, what so intoxicating, as possibility!"*
> **—Søren Kierkegaard**

Goals give you something concrete to focus on, and they typically have a positive impact on your actions. Goals help you focus your attention on your purpose so that it becomes your dominant aspiration. Seeing the invisible can do the impossible.

Once God gives us a vision, He works hard to lead us on the path He has prepared for us. Yet over and over again, we try to escape from the Master Sculptor's hand to pursue our own goals. God will never allow us to be satisfied with a goal that is lower than the path He has defined for us.

Goals help you focus your attention on your purpose...

> *"There is no passion to be found playing small, in settling for a life that is less than the one you are capable of living."*
> **—Nelson Mandela**

Short-term goals are important to get us going, but we also need long-term goals that encourage us to focus on the future. I think the expression that tells us to take it "one day at a time" is wrong. I think that stifles your creativity for drumming up business and causes you to think in the short term. I like to look at it as taking one week at a time, one month at a time, or one year at a time. You must have long-range vision to keep you from being frustrated by short-range failures. Someone said that only people who can see the invisible can do the impossible.

The most effective goals are SMART: Specific, Measurable, Achievable, Relevant, and Time sensitive. When you set goals and then

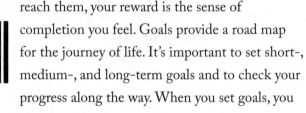

reach them, your reward is the sense of completion you feel. Goals provide a road map for the journey of life. It's important to set short-, medium-, and long-term goals and to check your progress along the way. When you set goals, you are planning to succeed. Goal setting should rank high in every professional's life. You can turn dreams into reality by setting good goals.

"The world makes way for the man who knows where he is going."
—Ralph Waldo Emerson

Live by the Compass, Not by the Clock

Once we set our goals, we need to keep the end game in mind and not get caught up in the details—the deadlines, the conflicting demands on our time, and the frustrating details. We have two options for how to manage our lives:

1. By the clock—by external forces like time commitments

2. By the compass—by internal forces such as your calling

We often struggle because there is a gap between the clock and the compass—when our actions don't contribute to the values we hold most dear. To help determine whether you are a slave to the clock or guided by the compass, take a few minutes to answer the following questions:

- What is my calling in life?

- What is my vision?

- What are my core values?

- What is my mission in life?

> *"We must all hang together, or assuredly we shall all hang separately."*
> **—Benjamin Franklin**

Build Alliances

Sometimes we need help to achieve our dreams. There is strength in numbers, so keep good company. Cultivate a group of talented, reliable, passionate people you can call on in tough times. Share your dreams with one another, whether this is a formal Board of Directors' meeting for a company or a close-knit group of personal friends and colleagues. Share ideas, support, and encouragement with one another.

> *"Take up one idea. Make that one idea your life— dream of it, think of it, live on that idea. Let the brain, the body, muscles, nerves, every part of your body be full of that idea, and just leave every other idea alone. This is the way to success ... "*
> **—Swami Vivekananda in Vedanta Philosophy**

Beauty in Distortion: Vow to Succeed, No Matter What

When I started out in sales, I was selling fire alarms for Interstate Engineering. In my first month, I had about twenty appointments but didn't close even one sale. I needed the money, so that was the only thing on my mind. My trainer told me, "You are selling from your pocket, not from your heart." To help me be more compassionate toward burn victims, he took me to the Burn Care Unit at Shriners Hospital in Boston.

When I saw the children, who had suffered severe burns from various types of accidents, it made me sick to my stomach. I was stunned. In that instant, I realized that some of the problems I had worried about over the years were insignificant compared to the battle for life these children were fighting.

A seven-year-old girl walked up to me and said, "My name is Susan. What's yours?"

I said, "Bobby."

This little girl had undergone seventy operations but was still disfigured. She asked me the most profound question I've ever heard: "Do you think I am pretty?"

I knelt down, so I could speak with her at eye level. I replied, "I think you're absolutely beautiful."

She asked me, "Why won't Mommy or Daddy hug me and kiss me anymore?"

I took a deep breath and said, "You see, Susan, your mom and dad feel really bad for what happened to you, and they blame themselves. But they love you more than anything, and that is why you are here, getting special care. Don't ever think that you are less than beautiful. You can be anything you want to be in life."

I hugged the little girl and kissed her on the cheek. She looked up at me with tears in her eyes and she said, "I really feel special now."

By the way, I successfully went on to become International Sales Champion for a Fortune 100 company—four consecutive times.

We must believe that, with God's help, we can do anything. The Beatles thought so! They sang, "Let It Be." Do you feel that you can do anything? Or have you given up on your dreams? Has life beaten you down? Do you feel that your dream is impossible? Success isn't always linear or flawless. Sometimes it takes a distorted path to get there. You can do anything you set your mind to. So what do you want to accomplish? What can you do every day that makes your heart beat faster? What goals will get you there? What is keeping you from getting started? Set out on your path to fulfill your God-given calling today, and vow to let nothing stand in your way.

"Keep a cool head and a warm heart."
—Mike Love

DENZEL WASHINGTON'S RULES FOR SUCCESS

Top 10 Drum Tips—How to Become the "One 2 Beat"

1. Dreams Need Goals

2. Aspire to Make a Difference

3. Ignore the Opinions of Others

4. Stick to Your Guns

5. Bring Your Dreams to Life

6. Share Your Gift

7. Work Hard

8. Fall Forward

9. Take What's Useful

10. Tell Great Stories

Before we move on to Beat 5, let's review the strategies we learned in this chapter:

1. Channel your passion through vision.

2. Lead through vision.

3. Use goals to accomplish your vision.

4. Live by the compass, not by the clock.

5. Build alliances.

6. Vow to succeed, no matter what.

BEAT
5

BIG BANG THEORY
New York Moxie

*"In this world a man must either be an anvil
or a hammer."*
—Henry Wadsworth Longfellow

"Moxie" is a word we hear a lot in New York City. You gotta have New York moxie. It means something or someone possessing the attributes of energy, pep, courage, determination, or "coolness"—the hallmarks of many New Yorkers like me. People with moxie are a lot more likely to drum up business than those who trudge through life with frowns on their faces and fear in their hearts. When you are full of moxie, people will look up to you and consider you the "One 2 Beat!"

*"I want to be the DH [designated hitter].
No base hits for me. Either give me all the
boos ... (or) Give me all the cheers!"*
-Bobby DelVecchio

You may have heard the expression from Tony Robbins, "Awaken the giant within. You should take immediate control of your mental, emotional, physical, and financial destiny!"

Well, I would like to make an expression that differs slightly, **"Awaken the *David* in you. Let *God* take immediate control of your mental, emotional, physical, and financial destiny!"**

Drumming Up Business

Conquer the giants in your life! In 1 Samuel 17 of the Bible, a boy named David hurls a stone from his sling and hits a giant, Goliath, in the center of his forehead. Goliath falls to the ground on his face, and David cuts off his head.

Not everyone has a giant within them, but we all have a David in us. It took great courage for this small boy to even think about confronting a powerful giant. The moral of this story is: a warrior's deadliest weapon is his mind. So, tell me, do you have the heart of a gladiator or that of a spectator?

Awaken the David in you.

Moxie means being quick. When my daughter was fourteen, I took her to a Broadway audition. The director called for someone to perform a particular part, and a swarm of girls darted to the stage in a New York minute. My daughter was left in the dust. The lesson learned: the early bird gets the worm. You've got to be aggressive, and you've got to go for it. This is about survival of the fittest, and only the strong (and quick) survive. The end of the story though, was what the director was about to ask; "Does anyone know the song 'Tomorrow'?" Of course, all those overly-eager teens didn't, and my daughter ended up getting the part.

Moxie means exhibiting intense passion. Tom Landry, the former coach of the Dallas Cowboys, once commented on the walk-ons who showed up each spring to try out for the team. Talent, he observed, was in abundance. Intense passion and desire were not. We are to make constant moral and spiritual progress similar to an army that is steadfastly marching toward its objective— Determined ... Progressing ... Undaunted ... like a Roman gladiator.

"Cui cerca, trova; cui secuta, vinci."
(Who seeks, finds; who perseveres, wins.)
-Sicilian Proverb

Adjust to Meet the Demands of the Changing Business Climate

"The Times They Are A Changin.'" Our parents told us that if we landed a good entry-level position at a major company, we would be set for life. They said, "Simply do your job, and maybe put in a bit of extra effort, and you'll be rewarded with annual pay raises." But in the brave new world, it takes more than just showing up and doing a little extra to make it big. The ones who will rise to the top are the movers and shakers—the entrepreneurs and innovative thinkers who make things happen.

September 11, 2001 was the beginning of a brave new world in American history. Just about every American remembers exactly how the terrorist attacks unfolded—where they were and what they were doing on that terrible morning of 9/11. According to an article in *Psychology Today*, the most significant effects of terrorist attacks such as the horrific one on 9/11 are economic in nature. The author notes that such attacks give us the impulse to avoid risky situations and be safe because we want to regain control of our lives. But such attacks also motivate us to seize the day and enjoy life to the fullest because we know our lives could change in a moment. Research has shown that consumers typically change their buying behavior after incidences of terrorism. For example, they often shop online instead of going to stores or malls. And after 9/11, people ate and entertained at home more often, causing restaurant sales to decline (Dholakia 2015).

We still ponder the questions raised by those attacks: What changed that day? What remains of the old? What is truly new?

As we examine these and other questions, we sense a turning point in our lives and in the way we do business. The challenges and dangers of international business expansion stand to multiply with threats of terrorism, diminishing revenue, increased competition, the dizzying pace of technological advances, and cyber-attacks that compromise information security.

Where is this all going? What can you do about it? Business owners and corporate managers must rethink every aspect of their operations in light of the new risk-management equation. Success in drumming up business requires a combination of Old World charm and New World ideas on the part of the business owner. Many years ago, I was given the nickname "Ambassador to the Franchisor." A franchise candidate once asked me, as I was negotiating a franchise agreement for a company I represented, "Who do you work for—me or the franchisor?"

I replied, "Without you, there is no franchisor." The bottom line is the individual business owner is what makes the world go 'round. In our personal and professional lives, we are to make constant moral and spiritual progress, similar to an army that is steadfastly marching toward its objective, similar to the boy who defeated the giant, determined and undaunted. Whatever natural or man-made disasters occur, we must adjust the way we do business to continue thriving in the new business climate.

> *"How beauteous mankind is! O brave new world that has such people in it!"*
> —*William Shakespeare,* **The Tempest**

Learn How Others Have Risen to the Top

In the old days, a big part of business success was developing commercial relationships and keeping up to date with developments in your industry sector. Well, guess what? In today's brave new world, it's even more important. The speed of business is increasing all the time, with new technology changing things far more quickly than in the past. The downside, of course, is that things can also go wrong far more rapidly. With the switch to a service economy, it's no doubt easier to start a company. But the statistics show that it's more difficult to achieve success over the long term.

The success rates of businesses in the private sector in America have been consistent over time. According to the US Bureau of Labor Statistics, about 80 percent of businesses with employees will survive their first year in business, about 66 percent of businesses with employees will survive their second year in business, and about half will survive their fifth year in business (Dholakia 2015).

The longer-term outlook isn't as good, only about 30 percent of businesses will survive their tenth year in business Statistics for franchising are the total opposite: 95 percent of franchises succeed in business (Otar 2018).

People who are highly competent have some things in common:

1. They are committed to excellence. Success should not be based on a comparison with others. Excellence gauges are valued by measuring us against our own potential.

2. They never settle for average. The word mediocrity literally means halfway up the stony mountain, and competent people never settle for average or mediocre.

3. They pay attention to detail.

4. Dale Carnegie said if you do the little things well, the big ones tend to take care of themselves.

5. They perform with consistency, and highly competitive people give their best all the time.

6. It is vital for new business owners to learn lessons from those individuals who have endured both failures and triumphs in their quest for success.

It would be naïve to believe that successful entrepreneurs made it because of luck. In fact, they've all encountered hurdles and hardships along the way. Here are some effective ways to learn from other successful people:

Surround yourself with great people.
When you're around great people, you will strive to be the best "One 2 Beat." It rubs off, I promise!

Read books or listen to audiobooks.
A lot of successful people have shared their stories about beating the odds to become champions. We all have a lot to learn by simply applying their hard-earned wisdom to our own lives. In a self-help world, some people think all we need is the latest book about overcoming whatever obstacle we are facing. That's why the self-help section of bookstores is so packed. It's not that simple, but we can benefit from observing the successes and the mistakes of others.

Listen to great speakers. The more you hear, the more you will have the desire to be like them. Go to seminars. If you don't walk away inspired by a great talk, then you probably shouldn't be in the game.

Set goals for yourself.
As we discussed in Beat 2, no matter how small the goal, it gives you something to strive for and a sense of purpose in life. Life is more fulfilling when you're moving forward.

Take some classes or lessons.
Whatever our level of experience, lessons always seem to inspire us. You will find new approaches, viewpoints, and techniques that you may have never encountered otherwise. Even the greats will often go back and study with a teacher after a long, successful career. They constantly

set and strive to reach goals in their lives and thrive on motivation, excitement, and competitiveness.

> *"Big shots are only little shots who keep shooting."*
> —**Christopher Morley (1890-1957)**

The Eye of the Tiger: Focus on Being the Best

Many business people are just going through the motions— doing just enough business to get by, but not thriving. Today's competition is tough. It takes guts to be the best. There is no excuse for lacking passion in whatever you're doing. Make it your goal to rise up the ranks of the ordinary and stand out. Be the best in your field. Be the "One 2 Beat."

In the third *Rocky* movie, Rocky Balboa is said to have "the eye of the tiger." In fact, the band Survivor wrote the song "The Eye of the Tiger" at Sylvester Stallone's request, to be featured in the film. The phrase refers to a complete focus on being the best, and that's what made Rocky a winner.

The Bible also tells us to be winners::

> *"The LORD will make you the head, not the tail. If you pay attention to the commands of the LORD your God that I give you this day and carefully follow them, you will always be at the top, never at the bottom."*
> —**Deuteronomy 28:13**

Maybe it's my passion for life and a focus on accomplishing goals and getting the job done that motivated me to be all that God created me— and to be the head instead of the tail.

Build Your Soft Skills

In past decades, success in business was often attributed to hard, or technical, skills and knowledge. Hard skills include statistical analysis, software development, data mining, and marketing. Today, success in business depends on soft skills, which are not measurable, but are critical in drumming up business. Soft skills include communication, the ability to manage emotions, leadership, adapting to change, having sense of humor, enthusiasm and problem solving. In fact, a recent study from Boston College, Harvard University, and the University of Michigan found that training employees in soft skills such as communication and problem-solving boosts productivity and retention 12 percent. It also delivers an amazing 250 percent return on investment because it leads to higher productivity and retention (Adhvaryu 2017).

Soft skills are a must today because companies need to become more dynamic, interconnected, and flexible. According to Deloitte's 2016 Global Human Capital Trends report, 92 percent of Deloitte's executives rate soft skills as a critical priority because they foster employee retention, improve leadership, and build a meaningful culture (Bruce 2017). They noted that a human resources leader's mission has shifted from that of "chief talent executive" to "chief employee experience officer." The great news is that people can learn soft skills. Three of the most important soft skills in today's business environment are emotion control, problem solving, and purpose—feeling connected to a mission beyond ourselves and our own self-interest.

My favorite sale closing lines: "Can you see where … ? Are you interested? … When do you think would be the best time to start?" These questions apply to almost any product or service you sell. If they say "no" or they want to think about it, say, "If you were to do it, why would you?"

*"Think twice before you speak, because
your words and influence will plant the seed
of either success or failure in the mind of
another.*

—Napoleon Hill

Some of the most important people in my life have told me the
importance of "soft skills" for years. Dr. NakaMats is the world's greatest
inventor; he has more than 3,500 inventions to his credit. He once told
me that the number one ingredient for obtaining success is persistence.
My mother once told me that success for a musician is defined by three
key components: talent, skill, and motivation. Talents are those gifts we
are born with, such as intelligence, while skills are those things we learn
through practice, and motivation is more about attitude.

Today's buzzword is "integrity." When I was growing up with
my Italian family, it was called "respect." Whatever you call it, it is a
critical skill in building rapport and trust with prospects. A professional
appearance and demeanor are critical, too. If you act professionally at
all times, chances are you will be treated in a professional manner. Treat
your job like an important part of your success and future, not like a big
party. Dress appropriately, and be clean. Stay sober, and be reserved, not
loud and boisterous. This is not to say you can't enjoy yourself, though. If
we didn't enjoy our work, life would be a drag. But take care of business
first. The better you perform your job, the more you will enjoy your work,
and the more respect you will get. All these important characteristics that
cannot be measured are critical to excelling in business in today's brave
new world.

"Nothing in this world can take the place of persistence.

Talent will not: nothing is more common than unsuccessful men with talent. Genius will not ... Education will not; the world is full of educated derelicts. Persistence and determination alone are omnipotent."
—Calvin Coolidge

Most successful people go through apprenticeship or a period of seasoning. Some people are recognized early in their career for their great potential and are groomed to succeed. Others labor in obscurity for years—learning, growing, and gaining experience. Then after a decade of hard work, they become "overnight successes."

Given the right encouragement, training, and opportunities, nearly anyone with desire has the potential to emerge as an impact player.

Choose to Be Uncommon

The following creed was written by Dean Alfange. It aptly sums up my feelings about not giving in to status quo.

I do not choose to be a common man.
It is my right to be uncommon ... if I can,
I seek opportunity ... not security.
I do not wish to be a kept citizen,
Humbled and dulled by having the State look after me.
I want to take the calculated risk;
To dream and to build.
To fail and to succeed.

I refuse to barter incentive for a dollar;
I prefer the challenges of life
To the guaranteed existence;
The thrill of fulfillment
To the stale calm of Utopia.
I will not trade freedom for beneficence
Nor my dignity for a handout.
I will never cower before any master
Nor bend to any threat.
It is my heritage to stand erect,
Proud and unafraid;
To think and act for myself,
To enjoy the benefit of my creations
And to face the world boldly and say:
This, with God's help, I have done.
All this is what it means
To be an Entrepreneur.

To have moxie means to set yourself apart from everyone else. It means establishing yourself as the "One 2 Beat."

Ways to Get Your Mojo Back (Yeah, Baby!)

Occasionally in life we are "Rocking and Rolling" and everything seems to be going our way. Then all of a sudden, we get blind-sided with an unfortunate circumstance that throws us off balance, and we lose our momentum, confidence, and well-being. It seems to be impossible to get yourself back on track—you lost your Mojo!

Here are some tips I've learned to get back in the "Groove":

Change Your priorities

I've found that putting God in the center of everything I do transforms my relationships, my work, my play, and my health.

Change your viewpoint

When you realize this hard place will pass and you give thanks for what you have now, you will start feeling better about yourself.

Change your attitude

Zig Ziglar would say, "Attitude makes Altitude." You can and will rise above your situation. You've just got to get on "The good foot."

Change your friends

You are the average of the five people you hang out with. Someone may be lowering your average. Reevaluate your "entourage" and make necessary adjustments.

Change your activities

I found that when I'm feeling down, I listen to music to put me back in "The Mood." Also, reach out to people in need. When you help other people with their problems, you start feeling better about yourself.

> *Remember, "You get everything you want in life, if you help enough other people get what they want."*
> *—Zig Ziglar*

Succeed Even If You Are Different

My sharpness does not come from a blade of a sword; my sharpness comes from within.

Sometimes people shrink back and live quietly because they think they are not meant to succeed. Often, it's because they are different from everyone else. My daughter, Daira, recently wrote a blog post about the unique challenges and opportunities associated with being a "girl boss." Her article is full of New York moxie. It's all about embracing your differences and excelling based on your unique talents.

Here is an excerpt from her blog post:

> It seems that the trend of "girl bosses" is everywhere nowadays, and I'm OK with it. (I am the guilty owner of a mug that reads "Just a Girl Boss Building Her Empire.")

> Anything that inspires women to be empowered is a message that the world could use a little more of. However, I have also found that being a girl boss isn't as easy as owning some memorabilia or walking overconfidently through a local mall. Being a girl boss actually means that you have some challenges that are different from being a guy boss.

> And guess what? The sooner you embrace what it means to truly be a girl boss, the more unstoppable you will become.

Daira goes on to say that women shouldn't feel like they need to act like men to succeed; in fact, she says, "There is strength in being vulnerable."

So, if you are different from the "average" salesperson out there, think of it as an advantage. You don't want to be like everyone else anyway.

Be a Master Lead Generator

If you want to drum up business better than anyone else—if you want to be the "One 2 Beat" in this area—then become a master at lead generation. This means you can't do what everyone else is doing. Everyone else is going to trade shows or franchise shows and picking up a few leads. Someone told me once, "I got five hundred leads last week at a franchise show. How many leads did you get?"

I replied, "I got four thousand leads."

The salesman told me, "You're just one person; how'd you do that?"

"Well, I got to where the money is. While you guys were doing the franchise show and competing with two hundred companies there, I went to the boat show, where there were no other franchise companies, and I got leads from people who can afford yachts. I figure if they can afford a yacht, they probably are either doctors, lawyers, or high-level executives. And maybe they're looking to buy a business. Many of them are retired."

Another way to multiply your sales through lead generation is to teach your entire staff the best sales strategies—not just your salespeople, but your receptionists and administrative assistants, too. They are the ones who work with customers every day on the phones and in the office. I once met a guy who owns a chain of muffler shops, and he had a total of twelve hundred employees. He said to me, "So, are you going to help me drum up more business?"

I said, "No, I'm going to help your twelve hundred employees drum up more business, and you should probably sit in, too. You'll probably learn a few things."

Always Ask for Referrals

In the music business, you're only as good as your last hit record. In sales, you're only as good as your last sale. When Zig Ziglar was training me, I walked in one day, and he asked, "How'd you do on that appointment?"

I said, "I got the sale."

"Congratulations! How many referrals did you get?" I said, "I got ten referrals."

He reached his hand out to shake mine and said, "Well done. See, you already spent the money that helped you get that sale, and now those referrals will fund your future sales."

The next time you're not happy with new leads or sales, look at yourself in the mirror and ask, "Am I asking for referrals?" Getting good referrals increases your sales with a lot less effort than it takes to get sales from "cold" leads.

As you know, it takes a lot of time and effort to build relationships to the point where people trust you enough to buy from you. With referrals, your most loyal customers tell other people how happy they are with your products or services, so those people come to you without your having to spend all that time up front.

You should always ask for referrals. Here are some tips on how to do it:

1. Ask for referrals when customers tell you they are happy with your service.

2. Run a referral-based organization—require everyone to ask for referrals.

3. Let people know how much you value those who refer others to you.

4. If a customer doesn't give you a referral, share a testimonial from a highly satisfied customer.

Your conversation with an existing client can go something like this: "My goal is to make sure you are 100 percent satisfied. Why don't you get your address book so we can put my number in it?

"Now that you have your address book out, who can you think of with your qualities who could possibly benefit from having an energy evaluation? I will contact anyone you mention personally and treat them with the same respect as I have treated you."

If you sell tangible products, recognize that the customer is happiest the day the product is delivered. Visit the job the day after the installation, and do the following:

1. Do a satisfaction inspection, and ask for referrals.

2. Take photos, and ask for testimonial letters to put on your website and in other marketing materials.

3. Ask new clients who were referred to you to thank the person who put you in touch with them.

Be Ultra-Creative in Your Marketing

Just as you need to be unique in your lead generation approach, you also need to be unique in your marketing approach. Do what no one else has thought of yet.

Dr. NakaMats, the number one inventor in the world, invented a putter that is five times more accurate than the Ping putter. He built a robot and studied velocity, drag, and angle. He finally perfected it.

I asked him, "What's so great about your putter?

He said, "It cures the yips." I'm not a golfer, so I had no idea what he was talking about. I thought it was a disease or the hiccups. I asked him what "yips" are.

Dr. NakaMats replied, "It's nervousness when you push or pull your putt. If you turn your wrist to the left, you're pulling the putt, and the ball will go to the left. If you turn it to the right, you're pushing the putt, and the ball will go to the right."

"So, in other words, it stops you from twisting your wrist?"

"Yes," he said.

"So come up with a strategy, a plan, an advertisement to let golfers know my putter cures the yips."

I said, "OK, I got it."

I had Dr. NakaMats fly with me from New York to Philadelphia. I called this guy I know who is extremely famous and said, "Meet me at the King of Prussia Golf Course." I had been the drummer for Chubby Checker, so I called him up that day to see if he would do a favor.

"I don't golf, Bobby."

I said, "That's OK. I don't either, but meet me there. I need to use you for an advertisement."

When he arrived, I took him into the pro shop and bought him a pair of red pants—he's kind of flamboyant—a white T-shirt, a golf glove, and a cap. I took him out on the green. I had photographers there. As they were about to snap a photo of him with Dr. NakaMats's putter, a women's golf team walked up. They had to be in their fifties, and they were all wearing matching skirts and tops. There were about fifteen of them.

One woman said, "Oh my God, look who it is!"

I said, "Women, would you do me a favor? Stand in a semi-circle behind him, so it's sort of like he's looking at the camera with a big smile, almost swinging the putter back, and you're all behind him like you're his big fans."

The photographers snapped some photos. I sent them to a magazine, and it appeared on the front cover of *Golf* magazine, *Golf*

Digest, Golf Shop Operations, Sports Illustrated, and *USA Today*. The caption read, "Even Chubby Checker won't twist his wrist with Dr. NakaMats' putter."

People saw the photos, and of course they recognized Chubby Checker. And they saw Dr. NakaMats's putter, which would keep a golfer from twisting his or her wrists, a problem just about every golfer has. Someone from the *Golf Digest* headquarters called us

and asked us to travel to Connecticut, so they could interview us about this new putter that Chubby Checker was advertising. Before long, everyone was describing Dr. NakaMats's putter like this: "Even Chubby Checker won't twist his wrist."

Then we flew to Miami to attend the PGA convention, the biggest golf convention in the world. Dr. NakaMats and I were both carrying one of his new putters in our own bags. When we showed up at the gate to board the airplane, there were two guards at the door. One of them asked, "What's in the bag?"

Being the New York wise guy that I am, I replied, "They're secret weapons."

The guards drew their guns, and we put our hands in the air. Everybody was looking at us. Dr. NakaMats was turning white, wondering if they were going to kill us or put us in jail.

I said, "No, no, it's just a golf putter. It's a golf putter."

They finally checked it out and let us go in. One of them said, "Don't say secret weapon, OK?"

Dr. NakaMats—one of the smartest living human beings— turned to me and said, "You're a genius. We are going to name it 'Dr. NakaMats's Secret Weapon.'"

After that, I never showed the putter in any of the magazines. I just showed the bag. And the caption read, "This putter is so dangerous to your opponent, that we can't reveal it here." People were buying the putter without ever seeing it. I had one hundred golf reps selling the putter, and we called them Secret Agents because they were selling "secret weapons."

What can you do to make your product or service stand out? What kind of outrageous but relevant strategy can you think of to differentiate yourself?

What can you do to make your product/service stand out?

"With a Little Help From My Friends"

Mentally strong people have healthy habits. They manage their emotions, thoughts, and behaviors in ways that set them up for success in life.

Face Obstacles with Courage

Here's another Band Story: We thought we hit the Big Time when we got an offer to play the famed Peppermint Lounge in New York City. What an experience! One of our favorite bands was Paul Revere and the Raiders; we loved the way they dressed in military jackets and tall, black boots. My dad had an idea. He gave us Marine Corps jackets, along with white pants and tall, black boots; we thought we were cool. Our opening debut, we played our hearts out. Then it began, the heckling came from a group of young Marine recruits, calling us names and accusing us of defaming the Marine Corps because we were wearing their uniform and having long, "Beatle-like" hair. The advantage of having microphones is that we could answer back and put them down, so the whole audience started laughing.

That didn't go over very well with these young crew cut recruits. A fight broke out, but we had an advantage; guitars to swing, mic stand to hit with, and drumsticks to poke with (of course my dad jumped in to help his boys—he was a boxer). We won the battle! My dad felt bad for what we did to these young men and bought them a round of drinks. He told them he was a Staff Sergeant in the Marines, and he gave us the jackets because we were playing Marine Corps bases to honor the Marines. These guys returned back every night for a week and told us if anyone gave us trouble, they would protect us.

I enjoy watching eagles play with the wind. They ride thermal updrafts to an altitude of fourteen thousand feet. The golden eagle can reach a speed of 180 miles per hour in a dive. "Those who hope in the Lord will renew their strength. They will soar on wings like eagles; they will run and not grow weary; they will walk and not be faint" (Isa. 40:31 NIV). Eagles travel light – their bones are hollow and filled with air. The seven thousand feathers on the bald eagle weigh only twenty-one ounces.

"Let us strip off anything that slows us down or holds us back, and especially those sins that wrap themselves himself so tightly around our feet and trip us up; and let us run with patience the particular race that God has set before us" (Heb. 12:1 TLB).

Some people avoid making improvements that are costly and that require self-denial, self-restraint, and self-sacrifice, but it is hard work and overcoming difficulties that ultimately lead us to greatness. It sometimes takes courage and faith to plow through the obstacles to success. We all deserve a standing ovation at least once in our life!

"I learned that courage was not the absence of fear, but the triumph over it. The brave man is not he who does not feel afraid, but he who conquers that fear."
— Nelson Mandela

Do you have the faith to believe you can overcome trials with God's help? Or are you paralyzed by indecision, over-analysis, and paralysis? Do you have the courage to believe that failure is not an option, that you will circumvent, tunnel through, or go over the obstacles until the mission is accomplished?

Hope is an important aspect of recovering. But it's faith that will get you through So, when I was diagnosed with throat cancer, I didn't say to God, "Pretty please, I hope I can get through this cancer." Instead, I said, "God I'm praying right now because with the faith that I have in you, I know I will get over this cancer." And I did. Having faith is New York moxie!

> **"Hope goes through the fire. Faith leaps over it."**
>
> **—Jim Carrey**

Let's look at the difference between an eagle and a chicken. Eagles soar in the sky, gaining altitude to see the big picture. Once they spot their prey, they drop down with lightning speed to accomplish their mission of procuring their next meal.

Eagles have keen eyesight; they see eight times better than human beings. They can spot a mouse in the grass a mile away. "The eye is the lamp of the body. If your eyes are good, your whole body will be full of light. But if your eyes are bad, your whole body will be full of darkness. If the light within you is darkness, how great is that darkness" (Matthew 6:22 BSB).

Eagles are focused. Once the eagle has spotted its prey, it does not take its eyes off the creature until it strikes. "But One thing I do: Forgetting what is behind and straining toward what is ahead, I press on toward the goal for which God has called me heavenward in Christ Jesus" (Phil. 3:13–14).

The eagle prefers peace and quiet when raising a family. They build their nests in the high hard-to-reach areas. "Make it your ambition to lead a quiet life ..." (1 Thess. 4:11).

Eagles, male and female, work together in building their nest; the arduous task takes several weeks to several months. "Two are better than one, because they have a good return for their work: if anyone falls down, his friend can help them up. But pity the man who falls and has no one to help him up" (Eccl. 4:9–10).

Eagles keep improving their home. They continue to bring fresh green sprigs through the nesting. Some think the sprigs are simply for decoration. "Blessed are those whose strength is in you, whose hearts are set on pilgrimage. As they pass through the valley of Baka, they make it a place of springs" (Psalm 84:5–6). Eagles fiercely defend their nestlings. They stand up against any animal that might be a threat to their young. "I am the good shepherd. The good shepherd lays down his life for the sheep" (John 10:11).

Eagles mate for life, and the eagle takes the new mate only if the first mate dies.

Chickens, on the other hand, cluck, peck, strut, mill around, and lay eggs when the urge comes upon them.

Which are you? An eagle that rises above his circumstances, who brings vision, faith, and courage to a coordinated effort, or are you a business-as-usual chicken that struts around and clucks, performing only when the urge comes upon you?

> *"Do not pray for easy lives. Pray to be stronger men. Do not pray for tasks equal to your powers. Pray for powers equal to your tasks. Then the doing of your work shall be no miracle, but you shall be the miracle."*
> **—Phillips Brooks**

Persevere to the End

Even the tiny ant knows about strength. The great Oriental conqueror Tamerlane once told his friends this inspirational story: "I once was forced to take shelter from my enemies in a dilapidated building, where I sat alone for many hours. Wishing to divert my mind from my hopeless situation, I fixed my eyes on an ant carrying a kernel of corn larger than itself up a high wall. I counted its attempts to accomplish this feat. The corn fell sixty-nine times to the ground, but the insect persevered. The seventieth time, it reached the top. The ant's accomplishment gave me courage for the moment, and I never forgot the lesson."

Advice from María Sabina, a Mexican healer and poet:

> Heal yourself with the light of the sun and the rays of the moon. With the sound of the river and the waterfall. With the swaying of the sea and the fluttering of birds. Heal yourself with mint, neem, and eucalyptus. Sweeten with lavender, rosemary, and chamomile. Hug yourself with the cocoa bean and a hint of cinnamon. Put love in tea instead of sugar and drink it looking at the stars. Heal yourself with the kisses that the wind gives you and the hugs of the rain. Stand strong with your bare feet on the ground and with everything that comes from it. Be smarter every day by listening to your intuition, looking at the world with your forehead. Jump, dance, sing, so that you live happier. Heal yourself, with beautiful love, and always remember … you are the medicine.

To have moxie means to face difficult times with strength and persistence, which ants demonstrate so well. As humans, we are capable of so much more!

To be the "One 2 Beat," face life's inevitable setbacks with moxie. Become known as the person who never gives up but braves the storm and not only survives but thrives.

MARTIN LUTHER KING'S RULES FOR SUCCESS

Top 10 Drum Tips—How to Become the "One 2 Beat"

1. Be Bold

2. Do It with a Full Heart

3. Challenge Yourself

4. Be Creative

5. Keep Moving

6. Have Energy

7. Enjoy What You Do

8. Have a Sense of Humor

9. Follow Your Dreams

10. Inspire Other People

Before we move on to Beat 6, let's review the strategies we learned in this chapter:

1. Adjust to meet the demands of the changing business climate.

2. Learn how others have risen to the top.

3. Focus on being the best.

4. Build your soft skills.

5. Choose to be uncommon.

6. Succeed even if you are different.

7. Always ask for referrals.

8. Be a master at lead generation.

9. Be ultra-creative in your marketing.

10. Face obstacles with courage.

11. Persevere to the end.

BEAT OF A DIFFERENT DRUMMER
Leadership

"If a man does not keep pace with his companions, perhaps it is because he hears a different drummer. Let him step to the music which he hears, however measured, or far away."
—Henry David Thoreau

The phrase "to march to the beat of a different drum" means to do things one's own way, regardless of conventional societal norms and expectations. It originally came from the writings of the American philosopher Henry David Thoreau. Great leaders in all walks of life, in all disciplines, have echoed that phrase because they know that being a true leader takes bravery, to stand alone and face the giant in your life as David faced Goliath. Leaders must have not only a vision and communication skills, but also personal resolve. I once asked Dr. NakaMats what the definition of a leader is. He asked me to get a piece of string and put it on the table. Then he asked me to push the end of the string and asked, "Where does it go?"

I responded, "All over the place. In no specific direction."

Then he told me to pull the end and again asked me where it went. This time I responded, "Wherever I pull it."

"That is the definition of a leader," he said.

This story helped me see that it doesn't matter what your resources are; it's about how you use them. Leaders must use their existing resources and direct them in the right places with concentration and intention to succeed. You must be steadfast.

> **steadfast** \STED-fast\ adjective. 1. Firmly fixed or established; fast fixed; firm. 2. Not fickle or wavering; constant; firm; resolute; unswerving; steady. https://www.gutenberg.org/ebooks/29765

One day I was asked to attend a seminar at the Central Florida Association for Women Lawyers (CFAWL) at The Citrus Club in Orlando. After the keynote address, I was told, "Bobby, I heard that you were a motivational speaker."

I replied, "Actually, I'm not. I'm an inspirational speaker." They asked what the difference is.

I said, "If I motivate you today, I'll have to motivate you tomorrow and the next day, but if I inspire you, you'll go on forever."

They said, "We've got it, you go around and light fires underneath people."

I said, "No I don't. I look for people already on fire, and I pour gasoline on them."

Inspiration is something that you feel on the inside, while *motivation* is something from the outside that compels you to act. *Inspiration* is a driving force, while *motivation* is a pulling force. Some people believe that motivation is for lazy people because they cannot be bothered getting things done.

> **"I used to think that running an organization was equivalent to conducting a symphony orchestra. But I don't think that's quite it; it's more like jazz. There is more improvisation."**
> **—Warren Bennis**

Choose to Be a Leader

"Play chess, not checkers, in life's decisions."

-Bobby Del

It's true what they say: leaders aren't born, they're made. Although there are certain traits that will set you up to be a good leader, so much of it is about choice. Having the desire, discipline, education, skills, and ability to learn from your mistakes will set you up to become a good leader. In other words, to be a good leader, you first must make the choice to be a leader.

People today are desperate for leaders; they want to be influenced by someone they can trust, a person of good character. Commitment comes before anything else in a leader's life. Leaders possess these characteristics:

- They make a great commitment to a great cause.

- They don't let fear cloud their view of the future.

- They pray about everything God favors.

- They have courageous persistence.

- They move ahead despite the odds.

If you're facing a God-sized challenge, cultivating these characteristics gives you the edge. The greatest achievers and leaders remain confident regardless of their circumstances. Confidence is characteristic of a positive attitude. The first step to becoming a leader is to really make the decision to do so. You might find yourself in a position of authority at your workplace or in your community, but this doesn't necessarily mean you are a leader. There is a difference between being the *boss* and being a *leader*. Anybody can boss people around, but true leaders inspire those around them to strive to do their best. Sometimes people find themselves in positions of leadership because of crises or special occasions. But typically, people become leaders simply because they make the choice to pursue the role.

Once you have your vision in mind, don't lose sight of it. The future will hold so many opportunities to get you sidetracked from your vision. True leaders don't let the details distract them from the big picture. If your vision is particularly ambitious, it will take courage to keep from letting others convince you that it is unachievable.

> *"The one thing you have that nobody else has is you. Your voice, your mind, your story, your vision."*
> **—Neil Gaiman**

Know Yourself

> *"Why are you trying so hard to fit in when you were born to stand out?"*
> **—Ian Wallace**

In order to be a leader, you must take an honest look at yourself. Take an honest assessment of your strengths and weaknesses. This sometimes isn't easy, and you might not always like what you see. But there's no way to improve upon your weaknesses if you don't first acknowledge them. Don't let your weaknesses dishearten you. Everyone has them. Focus on your strengths and strive to make them stronger, as you work to improve upon your weaknesses.

> *"If you're not God, then your opinion doesn't matter and your approval is not necessary."*

"Keep a cool head and a warm heart."

Always Keep Improving

There are a variety of ways to approach self-improvement. Formal classes, self-study, journaling and counseling are all excellent ways to work on yourself. Developing self-awareness is a lifelong process. However, a preoccupation with perpetual self-improvement can be frustrating. How can you appreciate what you've accomplished if you're always focusing on what you have left to do? Generally speaking, you should strive to find a balance between doing what you do best and branching out into new areas where your skills might not be as strong.

> *"I never learned anything while I was talking."*
>
> **—Larry King**

Take Ownership of Your Work

Any leader knows that the first thing that inspires people to follow you is the display of mastery in your field. How can you expect anyone to trust you, if you don't know what you're doing? It's so important to know your skills and your job inside and out. After you have mastered your own job, having a solid understanding of your employee's tasks and how the whole operation runs is also extremely useful. You will be able to train others in their tasks, while keeping track of the bigger picture.

Take credit when credit is due, and take responsibility when things go wrong. When things go wrong, which invariably they will sooner or later, don't wallow in your failure, take steps to correct the situation, and move on quickly and efficiently.

"People buy into the leader before they buy into the vision."

—**John Maxwell**

Stay Focused on Your Vision

After you choose to become a leader, take some time to ask yourself, "What is the goal here?" What is the thing you are striving for, either for yourself or for your organization? Take some time to envision it—what does it look like? What will it take to achieve this vision?

Know Your Employees

Before you can lead people, it's crucial to know whom you are leading. Knowing other people's strengths and weaknesses is almost as important as knowing your own. It's also helpful to know what a person's experience is, as a newer hire will always require more oversight than a more seasoned employee. Once you know the people who comprise your team, you can work to develop team spirit. Build an environment where people's best qualities shine through and where people can work with one another to develop new skills and strengthen weaknesses.

Offer praise rather than criticism. This will create an atmosphere of productivity and freedom. By imparting responsibility to your employees, you will instill in them a sense of ownership in your vision.

Communicate Effectively

Good communication is the hallmark of a good leader. But communication doesn't just mean speaking, it also means listening. Making sure your employees feel, see, and hear it, is so important to a good working relationship. When you communicate well, you help your employees understand your vision and your goals. You also help them understand where they fit into the big picture and what their role is.

Be aware that much communication is non-verbal. What you say with your body language, your facial expressions, and the tone in which you speak is often more important than what you say. You should always strive to be open, genuine, and truthful in all your relationships. Good communication builds trust. Stick to your word and do what you say you're going to do. Keep commitments and promises. Strive to keep deadlines, and if you can't do something within the timeframe that you've established, be honest about your challenges and do the best you can to complete the task as soon as possible.

Treat People with Respect

How you treat people, your employees, your customers, your friends, and family, is visible to all who see you. Remember that the way you treat people gives subtle messages to other people, including your children, about what your values are.

Strive to treat people with dignity and respect, regardless of status, wealth, age, or attractiveness. Respecting people is reflected not only in how we treat people, but also in how we set up our work environments. Do they promote health and safety? Peace and cooperation? Does the business that you set up benefit not just your clients, but also your employees?

The family is the foundation unit of every society. People will always put their family above all, as they should, but if you build your company in a way that benefits the individual and their family, you will motivate your employees to strive on behalf of those they provide for.

Be a Caretaker

Regardless of whether your leadership position was given to you or taken upon yourself, know that the role of leader means you inevitably will have followers. Whether you like it or not, you are responsible for those who follow you. Even though being a leader might seem glamorous, it is often a role of sacrifice and service. Strive to rid yourself of your ego and think instead of what you can do to benefit those who follow your lead.

Develop traits and skills in yourself that you would like others to emulate, such as honesty, dedication, integrity, bravery, and diligence. When a person is making the decision to follow you or not, he or she is thinking about their own well-being. He or she wants to know that you are going to look out for their well-being as well as the well-being of those they care about. Leaders who are self-interested are often unsuccessful because their followers can feel this selfishness and are instantly wary. The ensuing lack of trust will create a tension that cannot be easily undone.

Know the Circumstances

People, projects, and situations are never "one size fits all." What works in one situation won't necessarily work in another. It's the job of the leader to consider an infinite number of factors and still come to concrete conclusions about how to move forward. Don't be afraid to take some time to step back and analyze a situation before you make choices. People will respect a thoughtful, considerate leader who has weighed many different perspectives, including their own, and can find solutions that work for everyone.

Find New Strategies

Often, companies rely on the old adage, "If it isn't broken, why fix it?" But our technology and lifestyles are changing so quickly, it's imperative that our businesses and business models change, so we can keep up. Instead of following models that already exist, true leaders find new methods of operating that ultimately change the rules of the game. While there's no sure-fire way to find innovative solutions to old problems, creative thinking can help you think outside the box and find new strategies and business models.

How old movies influenced me:

1. *West Side Story*—Bernardo (Black Jacket/Tie, Purple Shirt)
   East Side Story—Bobby DelVecchio (Black Jacket/Tie, Red Shirt)

2. *Rebel Without a Cause*—James Dean
   Rebel With a Cause—Bobby DelVecchio

3. *My Cousin Vinnie*—How I learned the art of negotiation! "Here are my options. Option a: I get my ass kicked, or option b: I kick your ass. I think I'm gonna go with option b: kickin' your ass."

4. *Cool Hand Luke*—"Cool Head. Warm Heart"

5. *Happy Feet*— Attitude!

6. *Gene Krupa Story*—"When I speak of natural drummers, I'm talking about guys that are playing with the talent God gave 'em."

7. *Nowhere Boy*—"Mom, why couldn't God have made me Elvis?" "Because He was waiting for you to be John Lennon."

8. *Across the Universe*—"Who you are is what you do."

9. *Rocky*—"Every champion was once a contender who refused to give up."

10. *Godfather*—"I'm going to make you an offer you can't refuse."

"Backward Thinking"

One day, my then four-year-old son asked me to play a game of who can finish a maze faster. We both grabbed a pencil and a maze book and started the clock. About thirty seconds into the process, my son said he was finished. I was only halfway through the maze. He said, "Do you want to try again?"

I said, "Yes, but let me pick the maze," (thinking he had done that one before). So, we started again, each of us racing to the finish line.

Ten seconds later, he said, "I'm done."

I was puzzled. How could my four-year-old beat me, an adult? Then he revealed his secret.

He said, "Dad, I just started at the end and went backwards. This way I could see all the roadblocks easier." What a twist on the old traditional strategy. He found a more creative way to see things and thus a quicker way indeed.

> *"When you do the common things in life in an uncommon way, you will command the attention of the world."*
> **—George Washington Carver**

Approach Your Work Creatively

There is never going to be one right approach to anything. Leadership requires vision, dedication, analysis, and compromise. But it also requires creativity. Over the years, I have learned from a variety of different leaders that creativity is the key to seeing things outside of the box and finding unconventional solutions. If you aren't

Leadership also requires creativity

creative, there are many different ways to increase creativity. Here are some suggestions:

1. **Develop your ability to observe.** Creative people see possibilities in everything and are constantly taking in information that becomes fodder for future endeavors. Try carrying around a notebook and jotting down interesting things you see.

2. **Follow your own schedule.** Creative thought doesn't have a day job; it doesn't keep a schedule. Be observant about the times of day that your best ideas come. Create a schedule for yourself that allows you to be open and present at those moments.

3. **Take time to be alone.** Before you can be open to new ideas, you have to overcome your fear of being alone. Creative ideas won't come if you are constantly surrounding and distracting yourself with other people. Sometimes it takes many dull hours for that one brilliant spark to come to you!

4. **Make limoncello from lemons.** (I'm Italian!) Rather than see your hardships as a detriment, think about how you can utilize your challenges to your advantage. Often it's these moments of greatest pain that produce the most fruitful growth and creative output.

5. **Embrace new experiences.** In order to have new thoughts, you have to shake up your routine with new experiences. Don't be afraid to fail; this failure will only be fodder for new ideas and experiences.

6. **Ask questions.** They say the unexamined life is no life at all. Strive to stay curious and expand your mind with thoughtful conversations and challenges, books, music, and movies.

7. **Watch people.** The only way to understand human nature is through observation. Take time to observe those around you.

8. **Don't fear failure.** If you are aiming high, it's inevitable that at times you will fail. Risk of failure is as much a part of creativity as the potential success.

9. **Follow your passion.** If you follow what you love, you are much more likely to succeed than if you are motivated by some external reward like money or recognition. This is because, ultimately, passion is a much stronger indication of commitment and drive.

10. **Daydream.** Taking some unscheduled time each day to dream. Just letting your mind wander is imperative to creativity. How can you know where your mind will take you if you never let it go?

11. **Prioritize the flow.** Learn what it takes to get into a state of concentration and calmness. Then, when you enter that state, don't let external constraints pull you out.

12. **Surround yourself with beauty.** Cultivate an artistic sensibility by surrounding yourself with things that make you happy. This will create a sense of peace and will also help you to understand what you like and don't like.

Do you know what the most powerful nation in the world is?

ImagiNation

Duplicating Yourself: Helping People Achieve Their Goals Through Business Ownership

In the world of business, franchising is the most successful business format. Did you know that 97 percent of all franchises opened during the past five years are still open? Compare that to the fact that less than 50 percent of non-franchised businesses are still open after the same timeframe. Why are franchises so successful?

Franchises are successful because they have created a time-tested and well-developed system for running a business. This system considers all aspects of running a successful franchise, and nothing is left to chance. The franchisor simply needs to follow the game plan, and they will be successful.

As an experienced business person rounding the corner into the next phase of your life, you may be looking out over the horizon for how to build a legacy for yourself and your family. After decades in a career, you have achieved much success through hard work and execution. You have followed your dreams and written a few chapters along the way. This speaks volumes to your abilities and the value that you created along the way in order to follow a path of your choosing.

However, you see that the time required to continue building your wealth is spent more on activities than on making your money and talents work for you. This is not acceptable, and you are taking time to reevaluate your next moves. As you stand at this crossroads, you are looking for an opportunity that will allow you to use your business talents, prior success, and business knowledge to create wealth and to build something that is yours.

Your driving force for investigating business ownership is manifold, but the foundation is that you want the freedom and independence of action found in business ownership. In essence, you are ready for an entrepreneurial venture, where the income is derived through interactions with customers. You are now looking for a business in which others can execute your plans and create value for you while you are free to pursue other endeavors. You also want to prove to yourself that you can succeed in a new venture and relish the adventure that this will entail.

These are the hallmarks of someone who enjoys achieving and proving to themselves that they can do whatever they set their mind to. Owning a successful business will give this feeling. The energy and drive you put into building your business will hopefully result in high income potential. You are looking for a business that will allow you to work with others and potentially expand to multiple units.

As you articulate your goals, they will serve as a good benchmark for investigating business models and speaking with franchise owners. These business people should have the same type of granularity in their goals. I believe this speaks to the caliber of franchise owners, and you will want to align yourself with peers whose orientation is similar to yours.

Now that you have started on this journey, you are looking out over the horizon and thinking about your long-term goals and how to create a strong work-life balance. While you have been well paid and achieved significant respect from your work colleagues, the value you created was mostly kept within the companies you worked for, as a result of your labor; it was not going to advance your financial security to the extent that you desire.

This is not meant to disparage the wealth that you have clearly created—I say this because we discussed that you are looking for something that can be grown to scale and then annuitized. At this stage in the game, many executives don't want to sell their life off in big chunks, and while they could undoubtedly find another executive position, this is not the direction to which you are most drawn. You envision a successful business as one that gives you the flexibility to make career and life choices as you see fit at the time of your choosing.

If you are a strong communicator, you may want to use this skill in building your business. Good communication will help you more easily develop a successful business that creates real value to customers as it provides desired products and/or services. Teaching and mentoring are all areas that you derive significant personal satisfaction from, so why not make them part of your business plan?

Your experience and systems implementation will give you a strategic advantage as you grow your new business. The lessons you learned about leading teams of people and organizing business processes will certainly pay off dividends when implemented in a new business, and your natural analytical tendencies will be well rewarded as you strive towards personally important goals. The ideal scenario will provide you with a business that will give you more flexibility and earnings so that you can enjoy more quality time with your family. You have always worked hard and will throw yourself into this endeavor, as you will enjoy the benefits of your efforts.

My involvement with ZGroup Franchising is committed to helping the people I work with realize their dreams. It doesn't make any difference to us which business you ultimately choose, as long as it is right for you. Remember, you don't need to settle. Trust your model and make sure that whichever choice you make is one you will be happy with for years.

I have personally sold over three thousand franchises in forty countries, during my thirty-five-year career in franchising. If you ever have a desire to explore owning a business of your own, contact: Bobby@ZGroupFranchising.com

Here is a comparison I made with my life experiences in the music and franchising industries, as it relates to picking the right franchise for yourself.

Drumming Up a "Hit" Record in Franchising

Prelude:
My music experience—how it relates to franchising
A Great Sound:
It's all in the mix—a balance of logic and emotion

The Band:

Producer—Franchisor

Engineer—Consultant

Musicians—Franchisee

The Song:

Hook—Is it memorable (catchy)?

Melody—Does it satisfy your interest?

Harmony—Do you relate/get along?

Arrangement—Franchise system.

Lyrics—Franchise agreement (FDD)

The Beat:

Does it feel right?

RATE-A-RECORD

A feature in the TV show, *American Bandstand*, was Dick Clark asking a boy and girl to grade up-and-coming hit songs on a scale of thirty-five to ninety-eight. One segment's young lady said, "It's got a good beat, and you can dance to it."

> *"It's a fascinating life and it's a reflection, probably, of my odd nature. I'm a case study for a Type A personality. I have a short attention span, I love activity, I'm into all sorts of strange and wonderful things."*
> **—Dick Clark**

PAUL MCCARTNEY'S RULES FOR SUCCESS

Top 10 Drum Tips—How to Become the "One 2 Beat"

1. Do It Because You Can't Help It

2. Be Different

3. Find Your Drive

4. Take It Step by Step

5. Just Get Out and Do It

6. Fight for Yourself

7. Produce What You Like

8. Find Your Creative Process

9. Have Integrity

10. Have Fun

Before we move on to Beat 7, let's review the strategies we learned in this chapter:

1. Choose to be a leader.

2. Stay focused on your vision.

3. Know yourself.

4. Never stop improving yourself.

5. Take ownership of your work.

6. Know your employees.

7. Communicate effectively.

8. Treat people with respect.

9. Be a caretaker.

10. Know the circumstances.

11. Find new strategies.

BEAT
7

PRACTICE MAKES PERFECT
Extraordinary Presentations

*"Practice does not make perfect.
Only perfect practice makes perfect."*
—Vince Lombardi

As a salesperson, you are, in essence, selling yourself. Your presentation, either one-on-one or on stage in front of an audience, is a direct reflection of what it will be like to do business with you. People buy from people they trust and relate to. You need to thoroughly understand your unique value proposition or presentation. What makes you different, and better, than your competition? Be able to answer this question in a compelling but not cocky way. Then practice describing your unique value proposition until it is second nature to you. If you appear nervous or lack confidence when you present your product or service to prospects, it will be difficult to drum up business.

Doing something over and over again is the only way to learn to do it well. In anything you do, if you repeat the position or motion the wrong way, it will create a bad habit. Anyone who has worked out or lifted weights knows that using the wrong technique can be damaging to your body.

When I taught my son, Sean, to drum, I'm sure it was boring for him at first. I had him practice a double stroke roll very slowly with the proper stick positioning for months at a time. I wanted him to develop the proper stick control and form. As a result, his playing became more controlled and faster. He developed style and grace.

There are many similarities between drumming and making extraordinary presentations. In both, practice is critical! Practice your presentation until it becomes second nature to you. That will allow you to maintain eye contact with your prospect or customer and study his or her body language instead of trying to figure out what to say next.

> *Tell me, and I forget.*
> *Teach me, and I remember.*
> *Involve me, and I will learn.*
> — **Xun Kuang, in the Xunzi**

Entertain Your Listeners

Have you ever attended a presentation or meeting that was dull, boring, and uncomfortable to sit through? Your main objective when that happens is to escape or to endure it by thinking about something more pleasant. To avoid that response when you are presenting, entertain your audience. Do these five things to keep your listeners engaged:

1. Make the conversation or presentation fun.

2. Keep your prospect engaged, both physically and mentally. Make the presentation as interactive as possible.

3. Act as if you already have the sale. Winners take responsibility; they offer no excuses.

4. Avoid telling people how great your product or service is. Telling is not selling. Telling is arguing. When you "tell" your prospects how wonderful your product or service is, they tend to resist.

5. Use positive statements. Words create images in people's minds, and if those images are negative, hearing them can cause the fight-or-flight instinct.

Instead of these negative words	Use these positive words
Contract	Agreement
Buy	Own
Sell or sold	Happily involved
Sign	Authorize
Payment	Investment
Pitch	Presentation
Price	Total investment
Monthly payment	Monthly investment
Cost	Investment
Deposit	Initial investment
Discount	Savings

Also, avoid using phrases like "to tell you the truth" and "let me be honest." They can make prospects and clients wonder, "So you weren't telling the truth or being honest during our other discussions?" Similarly, avoid saying, "trust me." It's better to earn people's trust by demonstrating ethical, professional behavior than by asking them to trust you.

Ask Questions to Keep Your Audience's Attention

There are some easy ways to hold your listeners' attention. This is true whether you are giving a keynote address or chatting with a potential client. One way to hold your listeners' attention is to ask questions. Here are different types of questions to ask; they all serve different purposes.

1. Open-Ended Questions

Ask open-ended questions at the beginning of your presentation to collect valuable information about your prospect's needs. These questions elicit detailed answers because they require more than a simple yes or no. An example of an open-ended question is, "What types of complaints do you have about your current provider?" Never ask open-ended questions in your close.

2. Closed-Ended Questions

Ask closed-ended questions in your close. These questions can be answered with a simple yes or no—for example, "Do you have any complaints about your current provider?" or "Do you want to move forward?"

3. Emotional-Involvement Questions

Emotional-involvement questions and comments create trust. They make your prospects feel good and ease them into their comfort zones. Here are some examples:

- I can see how you feel.
- The question you raised is valid and deserves some discussion.
- If I were you, I would probably ask the same question. Just to clarify my thinking …
- That's a very good question.
- So that I may give you the information you need, would you mind repeating your concern?

> *"People don't care how much you know until they know how much you care."*
> **—Theodore Roosevelt**

4. Reversal Questions

When you reverse a question, you answer a question with another question. He or she who asks the questions is in control. If the customers are asking all the questions, they are in control.

5. Hypothetical Questions and Comments

Hypothetical questions and comments allow you to consider "What if?" scenarios or potential alternatives with your prospects and clients. Using these questions is a great way to transition to the solution in the cycle of motivation. Here are some examples:

- What if ...?
- Let me ask you a question ...
- Let's pretend that ...
- Suppose you could ...

6. Possession Questions and Comments

Possession questions and comments put your prospect in possession of the product. Perception is reality. Build reality into the prospect's subconscious mind. For example, if you are selling solar panels, you could say, "John and Mary, how will you feel when your electric bill is a fraction of your current cost every month?"

7. Questions about Alternative Choices

During a conversation, you can control people's emotions by using questions. Remember, the person asking the question is in control.

"Sales is letting the other guy have it your way for the benefit of both parties."
-Bobby DelVecchio

Use a Trial Close to Gauge Your Prospect's Interest

A *trial close* is a great way to take your prospect's "temperature" while creating minor agreements and building momentum toward a final "yes." To use a trial close, ask the prospect a closed-ended question that requires him or her to give an opinion about your product or service, but not a commitment to own. You can turn any statement into a trial closing by using a "tie-down," which is a brief question you add to the end of a statement that leads the prospect to state an opinion. For example, in the following statement, "can't you?" is the tie-down: "You can see how this could make your life easier, can't you?"

Here are some more examples of tie-downs:

- Aren't they?
- Aren't you?
- Couldn't you?
- Don't you agree?
- Doesn't it?
- Don't you?
- Hasn't he/she?
- Haven't you?
- Isn't it?
- Isn't that right?
- Shouldn't you?
- Wouldn't you?
- Won't you?

"I just want to be perfect. And then what, you stop what happens when you achieve perfection? It's the imperfection that keeps us alive, motivating us to push further and further."

—High Strung (2016 film)

Practice Until You Are Comfortable

It's a tall order to expect to be perfect, but execute every technique as well as possible. Strive for excellence. This includes knowing your product or service, describing it with the proper timing, "reading" your prospects to gauge their interest level, being honest, and practicing, so you can achieve incremental improvement. We all enjoy what we're doing much more when we can see advancement and improvement.

> *"You practice like you play; you play like you practice."*
> —**Marcus Luttrell**

Here are some ideas to help make your practice sessions more productive and enjoyable:

- Maintain a positive attitude—"the good foot"—which is critical for peak performance.
- Sell as if your reputation depends on it.
- Practice at home, not on the job.
- Warm up before your presentation.
- Strive to constantly improve during each practice session.
- Try to be working on something new at all times.
- Never be satisfied.
- Vary your practice routine.
- Keep challenging yourself.
- Ask for feedback from people who will be honest with you (and have nothing to gain by flattering you).
- Videotape yourself presenting to an empty conference room.
- Work with a speech coach.
- Most importantly, be patient with yourself.

Concentrate on these tips only while practicing. Once you are making the presentation, don't think about them. Concentrate on the material and on feeling relaxed and comfortable. If you use these tips diligently every time you practice, you will find that they will creep into your presentation without you realizing it, and you will see a vast improvement in your delivery in a few short months.

Be a Storyteller

It's hard to imagine your career going anywhere if you can't tell a story. Whether it's an investor pitch, an "About Us" web page written for potential customers, a justification of your group's existence to management, or an "about me" description during an interview, your success in business is all about effective storytelling.

> *"We are what we repeatedly do. Excellence,*
> *then, is not an act, but a habit."*
> **—Will Durant**

There is a saying regarding practicing that has been attributed to the concert pianist Vladimir Horowitz and paraphrased by many. Here is one version: "If I miss one day, I know it. If I miss two days, my wife knows it. If I miss three days, my audience knows it." That is the consummate statement on the importance of regular practice.

> It's hard to imagine your career going anywhere if you can't tell a story.

The hours you put into practicing your presentation are very important in improving your closings. Much of the time spent rehearsing is often not put to the best use. Consider the old debate of quality versus quantity. If you focus on the right aspects of your presentation, you can accomplish more in thirty minutes than you can in two hours.

Many salespeople do not really practice; instead, they go through the motions of their presentations. They simply present what they know.

This can be great for the maintenance or polishing of certain techniques, but it won't help you progress or improve. Strive for improvement. While practicing, concentrate on being yourself. Be authentic.

Each practice session should create a challenge for you to accomplish something you've never previously done. The amount of practice time will vary according to your experience level. A beginning salesperson might practice thirty minutes to one hour a day and increase that to two hours per day. As you progress in your career and gain experience with selling, your practice time will decrease, but don't ever stop practicing! Be a lifelong learner.

There's an old saying that champions don't become champions in the ring. They earn their expertise through the quality of their practice sessions. Boxing is a good analogy for leadership development, because it is all about daily preparation. Even if a person has a natural talent, he has to prepare smart and train hard to become successful.

Use Storytelling to Sell Better

Telling compelling stories can help you get your funding, win the business, and get the job. Why is that? It's simple—media overload, communications overload, and gadget overload. These days, we're all overdosed with rhetoric. We are exposed to a thousand TV channels and movie choices, endless blogs and commentators, countless email blasts, and millions of websites. Each one is jockeying for a position in our lives, a share of our minds, and just thirty seconds of attention from our eyeballs.

Now, more than ever, if you can't tell a story in a way that grabs people's attention, gets across your position, causes them to relate to you and you to them, and sticks with them, you may as well just hang it up. It's as simple as that. Of course, a more positive way to look at it is that nothing can boost your career more or be more fulfilling than adeptly telling a story and truly connecting with your audience. Nothing.

Long ago, I was professionally trained as a speaker, I've given thousands of speeches and presentations, and I've been helping executives and companies position themselves, market their ideas, and tell stories for decades. I've also had the privilege of working for more than three decades with Dr. NakaMats. He has called me "an excellent storyteller."

Here are four main steps to telling a story and winning over any audience, with specific strategies in each step.

Step 1. The Set Up

You might have been taught to use your own point of view as the starting point of a presentation. Wrong! Dead wrong! Do you think companies are successful by making products they want to make, or by making products their customers want to buy? Do you think entrepreneurs get investment capital because they have a great idea or because it meets the criteria of their venture capitalists?

Here's how to make a presentation the right way.

1. **Determine who your audience is.** Don't even think of saying, "It's for everyone." That simply won't fly. If you can't specifically define your audience, you're sunk. If it's for multiple audiences, your presentation needs to be different for each one. I know it's a lot of work, but that's the way it works. If you dilute the message for multiple audiences, it won't hit any of them hard, and you'll fail to resonate with anyone.

2. **Put yourself in your audience's shoes.** The key is to relate to them and to give them the sense that they can relate to you. Ask yourself these three questions when you are preparing and making your presentation:

   • What's in it for them?
   • Why should they care?

- What criteria will your audience use to determine if whatever you are pitching is or is not a good idea?

Customers have very specific criteria they're looking to meet. Likewise, venture capitalists have specific criteria to determine if they should invest or not. This may take some research but trust me, it's worth it.

3. **Develop your story.** Of course, the story is all about what you are pitching. But if you don't put it in perspective for your audience and answer those three questions, you will never resonate with them. Also, consider the mechanics of the situation—that is, the time allotted for you to speak, the venue, and other variables.

Step 2: The Story

All effective, memorable stories have a beginning, a middle, and an end. Make sure yours do too. Depending on the situation, you can relate that to the old axiom, "First tell the audience what you're going to tell them, then tell them, and then tell them what you told them." Sometimes that's included in the story, sometimes not. Either way is fine.

If you are pitching potential customers, you can tell the story of how your product or service did something amazing for another customer and how that customer benefited by, for example, gaining market share or solving a costly problem. Again, say something dramatic that will resonate with the audience and answer the questions listed in the setup.

If it's an elevator pitch about your company, don't give the boring statistics. Don't say, "We're based in Toronto, Canada, we have six thousand employees, and our revenue last year was $1.4 billion." Instead, give a quick one-paragraph explanation of what your company does better than any other company, and then launch right into your biggest success story that will resonate with your audience.

If it's an interview and you're asked to tell about yourself, don't just rattle off the companies you've worked for and your accomplishments. If you truly know your audience, you can tell them a story from your experience that encapsulates the skills and traits they're mostly seeking.

If you are an entrepreneur who is pitching investors, your story could relate to the genesis of the idea, if it's an interesting or amusing story, and how it will change the world. If you can somehow relate it directly to investors as individuals by involving family or technology they use, that's good but not necessary. Just make sure that, somewhere along the line, you answer all the requisite questions that investors want answered before they write a check.

Step 3: The Delivery

Research and content are key, but don't skimp on the delivery. If you really want to engage your audience in an experience they'll remember— which means they'll remember your story— here are some tips to follow:

1. **Don't read what's on the slide.** If you're pitching from a slide presentation, don't read words off a slide. Instead, know the pitch cold (without having to look at the screen, except for a brief cue). Speak in your own words; don't recite a stiff quote from someone else.

2. **Don't block the audience's view.** Don't step in front of the screen or block it from view, except for the occasional walk across. Gesture with your hand, but don't touch the screen. Don't use a pointer unless you must.

   As an option, you can start with an icebreaker to break the tension (yours and theirs). It can be as simple as a welcome gesture or as involved as a brief and engaging or humorous anecdote. Above all, keep it brief, relevant, and appropriate.

After your optional icebreaker, tell your audience why they're there and what they can expect. This will relieve any tension or anxiety they might have if they're not sure what to expect. That will allow them to focus completely on your story. If you're absolutely sure they already know why they're there—maybe because somebody else provided a solid introduction, or they are attending a convention—then it's OK to dive right into the story.

Now it's story time. For the story to be memorable and to resonate with your audience, you have to make sure it delivers on what they came for. It needs to be dramatic in some way so that it evokes an emotional response. It helps greatly if you tell a story that comes from your own personal experience—from the heart.

3. **Engage the audience by asking questions**. If they don't respond, try offering an answer and asking for a show of hands, or ask easier questions. Make the audience part of the experience.

4. **Be accessible.** Don't stand behind a podium. Use a wireless mic if needed. Get close to the audience, and move from place to place while maintaining eye contact, but only from time to time. Don't bounce around like a ping-pong ball.

5. **Pause for effect and emphasis.** Practice being comfortable with silence for two or three seconds. It's the most dramatic way to make a point. Avoid saying "ah," "uh," "um," "so," and other fillers of uncomfortable silence; they are annoying and detract from your message.

6. **Make eye contact.** But do it only for only a few seconds per person. If eye contact is too short, you'll fail to engage. If it's too long, it becomes uncomfortable. Don't bounce your eyes around constantly.

7. **Use hand gestures.** They're engaging and interesting. But when you're not gesturing, keep your hands at your sides. Don't fidget, hold onto things, or put your hands in front of you, behind you, or in your pockets. Avoid making nervous movements.

8. **Don't overuse props.** The most important thing for engaging an audience and telling a memorable story is you, the storyteller. So, don't do too much to distract the audience from your own presence. I know it's a little scary at first, but you'll improve with practice and experience.

Step 4: The Close

The close is the easiest part to get right and the easiest part to screw up. I know that sounds contradictory, but it's not. Here's why. It's the easiest to screw up because, all too often, presenters forget to do it. They get so wound up in telling the story that they simply blow it. It's also the easiest to get right because the close is either telling them what you told them, as succinctly as possible, and/or driving home the one key point, the single message you want them to take away from your story or pitch. Simple, just don't forget to do it.

Your presentation is the most powerful marketing tool you have, so make it count! Make it represent your company and your product or service in the most favorable way possible. Make it extraordinary!

> *"If you stay ready, you ain't got to get ready."*
>
> **—James Brown**

DALE CARNEGIE'S RULES FOR SUCCESS

Top 10 Drum Tips—How to Become the "One 2 Beat"

1. Take a Chance

2. Be Enthusiastic

3. Learn to Love Your Work

4. Learn from Your Mistakes

5. Do Not Fear "FEAR"

6. Make Good Use of Your Time

7. Do Hard Jobs First

8. Be Persistent

9. We Determine Our Happiness

10. Remember, Everything You Do Sends a Message

Before we move on to Beat 8, let's review the strategies we learned in this chapter.

1. Sell yourself, and showcase your unique offering, with an extraordinary presentation.

2. Entertain your listeners.

3. Ask questions to keep your audience's attention.

4. Use a trial close to gauge your prospect's interest.

5. Practice until you're comfortable.

6. Be a storyteller.

TIMING IS EVERYTHING
Closing Execution

"You cannot be good all the time, you have to be good when it's time." One of the best advice René gave me.

—Céline

The drummer is the timekeeper of a band. He or she establishes the rhythm, pulse, and vibe of the other musicians and of the band's collective sound. The drummer's timing is critical. He or she must punctuate the melody at the exact, precise moment to deliver the most impact. Timing is a key part of execution. And that drumbeat doesn't exist until the drumstick hits the drum.

Someone asked me at a music festival once, "What kind of sticks do you use, 2B? 5B? 2A?"

I answered, "Tree branches, sauce spoons—anything I can beat the drums with."

Once, I even played a drum solo with two long-neck bottles of beer. You don't make a beat, get a sound, or make a statement until the stick hits the drum head. That is execution. A drummer, like a salesperson, is all about execution. There's no such thing as a close sale— close is only good in horseshoes and hand grenades.

The timing of a salesperson's close is critical, too, just as a comedian should have perfect timing and delivery. If you ask for the sale too early, before you have allowed the prospect to perceive your value and to establish that he or she needs what you're selling, you've botched it. If you are too timid and never ask for the sale, or ask too late, that's equally bad. Timing the steps to your sale just right will lead to flawless execution. All your product knowledge, experience, and preparation mean nothing, if you fail to time and execute the sale masterfully.

Read and Use Body Language Well

Communication is a huge part of making an initial good impression, which you must do before you can execute a sale. *What* we say, the content, is the least important part of communication; it makes up only 7 percent of our communications. Another 38 percent of communication is *how* we say it, and 55 percent is our *body language.*

You must project sincerity and confidence in your voice. Learn to use hand gestures (Italians do it all the time.), posture, and facial expressions as messages of positive reinforcement. And a genuine smile will go a long way toward sending out good vibes to your prospect.

Be Persistent

What separates the great salespeople from the mediocre? Persistence. Did you know that it takes, on average, at least eighteen calls to connect with a prospect over the phone? If you are giving up after the first, fifth, tenth, or even fifteenth try, you haven't even reached the average number of needed tries. Be persistent!

> *Your success is in direct proportion to the degree that you are able to overcome negativity and the temptation to give up.*

Are you willing to pay the price to achieve above average? Overcoming negativity is the price of achievement, the price of real success. Greatness is reserved for unusual success that only few achieve; many can be successful, only few become great.

Here are some of my thoughts about the value of persistence:

- Successful people do the things that unsuccessful people aren't willing to do.

- Miracles happen because of belief and persistence.

- I don't see failure as failure but as the game I play to win.

- Winning isn't everything, but the will to win is everything.

- Press on. Nothing in the world can take the place of persistence. Genius will not. Education will not. Talent will not. Nothing is more common than unsuccessful individuals with talent.

- Persistence and determination combined are omnipotent.

- Do high-priority work first. No excuses!

- Remember the 80-20 rule: Spend 20 percent of your time on the activities that will bring you 80 percent of your results. Concentrate your energy on what will give you desired results.

- Associate with individuals who have goals similar to yours.

- Each evening before I go to bed, I make a list of ten goals to be completed for the next day.

- Get up half an hour earlier than usual each morning, at least five days a week, and spend it reading or studying to enhance your professional skills.

- Create two distinct mission statements—one for business use and one for personal use.

- Make a list of personal affirmations, and read the list twice a day out loud.

- Do more than you're asked to do, and contribute more than is required of you.

- Persist. Persevere (Gonzales, 2020)!

- It's easier to be persistent and execute more sales when you are confident and efficient.

Seek Out Innovative New Ideas

I am the captain of my ship, the master of my fate, and God is my compass.

A leader can't possibly know enough or be in enough places to understand everything happening inside, and more importantly outside, your organization. But you can actively collect information that suggests new approaches. You can tap into a network of "listening posts" throughout the world. Knowledge gives you choices. The more options you know about, the more choices you have for moving your organization forward.

Don't just look at how the pieces of your business model fit together, but also at what doesn't fit. For instance, pay special attention to the marketing strategies of competitors, which are your best source of information about operational weaknesses or unmet needs. Also search out broader signs of change, such as a competitor doing something different and getting successful results.

"Set life's rhythm with your heart-drum."
—Johnathan Lockwood Huie

Create Perceived Value

Every sale begins with perceived value on the part of the prospect. If perceived value does not exist, you can't sell anything! It is up to you to create value in the prospect's mind. The prospect must perceive that your offering is a great value for them, and that happens when you make an extraordinary and masterful presentation.

People buy a product or service for the following reasons:

- They need it.

- They want it.

- They hope it will help them gain something.

- They fear that if they don't buy it, they will lose out.

You need to do the following things consistently and better than everyone else:

1. Dress for success. Your appearance is vitally important to your success. Because prospects are involved in helping you achieve your goals, you must be concerned with how they perceive you and your product or service.

2. Be prepared. As discussed in the previous chapter, practice your presentation until it's second nature to you.

3. Visualize a sale. See yourself succeeding.

4. Follow the basics.

5. Know your product or service.

6. Smile.

7. Be positive

8. Be sincere.

9. Tell the truth.

10. Don't sell—educate.

"Timing is essential for success."
- Bobby DelVecchio

Follow a Systematic Sales Process

Successful salespeople use a systematic approach to their sales. For new salespeople, it's the only thing that can replace experience. If you educate yourself on the system and practice it, you can be successful right from the start of your career. If you are a veteran, keep yourself tuned up with the steps, and you will sustain and improve your results.

Here is the process to a successful presentation:

1. Introduce your product or service.

2. Describe your qualifications.

3. Conduct a needs analysis.

4. Tell a compelling company or relevant personal story.

5. Create pain for the customer.

6. Offer alternative products or services.

7. Use one of three closes.

8. Execute the close.

9. Finish with the post-close.

10. Measure your results.

To achieve agreement with your prospect during each step of the selling process, the following must happen:

- The prospect will see the need.

- The prospect will desire the product.

- The prospect will feel it is affordable.

Emulate the Traits of Great Salespeople

Who are the best salespeople you know? Who makes selling seem effortless? Chances are the people who come to mind share these characteristics of successful salespeople:

1. Positive attitude. They do not allow failures or other events to affect their attitude. They are always positive and look to turn negatives into positives. They learn from their mistakes and don't dwell on them.

2. Creativity. Master salespeople use creative methods to develop practical solutions to overcome obstacles.

3. Persistence. This is different from insistence. One wins respect. The other annoys.

4. Vision. Great salespeople get excited about the future and make the most of their opportunities.

5. Integrity. People buy from people they like and trust.

6. Sincerity. Great salespeople are sincere in their interest in helping other people get what they want, and they get excited over the chance to serve people.

7. Conviction. The successful salesperson can talk to anyone and everyone with confidence.

8. Common sense. This trait enables you to solve problems and to come across to prospects as a logical, wise person.

9. Initiative. Great salespeople enjoy taking on the toughest prospects. They take on challenges that most salespeople would shy away from.

10. Belief in themselves. They expect to win and believe in themselves in every situation.

Nurture Strong Relationships Built on Trust

I've saved the most important strategy and concept for the end of this chapter because it is the anchor of every sale and every business: relationships. Your relationships with people, the trust and belief they have in you, will trump any other aspect of the sale.

Somebody asked me recently, "Why do you sell so much?"

I said, "Because I make friends with everybody, and people would rather buy from someone they like than somebody they don't like."

> Your relationships will trump any other aspect of the sale.

Here is an example of how important that is. I went to buy my wife a car, a 300ZX turbo. There were two dealerships one mile apart. I went to the first one and told the salesman what I wanted. After a lot of haggling, he said the price was $40,000. I negotiated the price down to $35,000, but he was arrogant and rude. He said, "Take it or leave it. If you walk out of here, the deal is off."

I said, "Really? OK, well, I'm going to leave because I'm not going to make a snap decision."

I went to the other place and asked how much the same car was. He said it was $40,000.

"Give me a deal."

He asked, "What do you want it for?"

And I told him I would pay $35,000 because I knew I could get it for that price down the street.

The salesman said he would sell it to me for $38,000. But he said, "I'll tell you what. If you buy this car, I'm buying it with you. If you have any service problems, you don't call the service department; you call me. I'm your personal concierge. Anything you want, you always come back to me because I want to build a relationship with you."

I signed the papers right there. My wife looked at me and said, "But it was three thousand dollars less at the other place."

"Yes, but they didn't have TLC."

She said, "What's that? Is that a special type of seatbelt?"

I said, "No, as my mother would say, tender loving care. Did you hear what the guy said? I don't have to call the manager, the service department, the warranty department. He's my personal concierge, and anything I need, I can go directly to him, and he'll take care of it."

That extra level of service was worth $3,000 to me because one service screw up will cost you a lot more than that.

Relationships are everything.

ZIG ZIGLAR'S RULES FOR SUCCESS

Top 10 Drum Tips—How to Become the "One 2 Beat"

1. Have a Dream

2. Think like a Champion

3. Be Committed

4. Do It Right Now!

5. Be Prepared

6. Keep Your Word

7. Set Goals

8. Evaluate Where You Are

9. Have Integrity

10. Don't Quit

Before we move on to Beat 9, let's review the strategies we learned in this chapter:

1. Read and use body language well.

2. Be persistent.

3. Seek out innovative new ideas.

4. Create perceived value.

5. Follow a systematic sales process.

6. Emulate the traits of great salespeople.

7. Nurture strong relationships built on trust.

I'VE GOT RHYTHM
Getting in Sync

"Music is the universal language of mankind."
—Henry Wadsworth Longfellow

Music and drumming benefit our health, our mood and our interactions with others. The combination of self-expression, discipline, fun, and working with others in a positive way is a winning combination for individuals as well as teams in a corporate setting. My aim is to reinforce that sentiment and to encourage you to want to make your "best music" in life and business.

The first sounds a baby hears while still in his or her mother's womb is the beating of her heart and the rhythm of her breath. Regardless of our race, gender, age, religion, or belief system, this common experience exists for all human beings.

> Music benefits our health, mood and interactions with others.

In fact, French researcher Franck Ramus believes that sensitivity to rhythm in babies may be an essential tool for the acquisition of language (Ramus, 2002). It's easy to assume that we develop a sense of rhythm and pulse with age and physical practice. We are all born with creativity and a desire to play with objects, ideas, skills, and concepts until they become second nature—yet we stifle these abilities through conservative actions and methods of learning. When adults are first introduced to drumming, they often say, "I don't have any rhythm," in an attempt to excuse themselves for their imagined inadequacy. But the truth is we all have rhythm!

Rhythm is Born

Known as the oldest instrument in the world, the drum is sacred and revered in African culture. For centuries, throughout the African continent, the drum was a primary source of communication. And, despite attempts to silence it, the rhythms of African drumming overcame slavery to emerge as the most influential drumming music in the Americas.

Slaveholders recognized the power of the drum to unite slaves; many slave traders and plantation owners banned drumming, fearing that slaves might use drums to organize and rebel. The drum was understood to be an instrument of communication. Since drums could "talk," they could be used to gather slaves together to plan rebellion. Slave owners sought to prevent African slaves from signaling for rebellion with their drums. Shaken by the1739 Stono Rebellion, the South Carolina colonial assembly outlawed hand drums the following year.

In a similar colonial context, as early as 1696 the legislature of Jamaica passed a law against gathering and drumming. The law was enacted to prevent resistance to the slave system.

"Oh, give me the beat, boys and free my soul"
—Dobie Gray

But You Can't Keep a Good Drummer Down

Even with these instances of the banning of drumming in colonial contexts, there is evidence that in some locations within early America drumming was not forbidden because it was not viewed by whites as a threat, or it continued in spite of any type of ban. The British museum received an African drum acquired in Virginia as part of the Sloane Bequest of 1753. The British believed it to be an Indian drum. It appears to be an Akan-style drum made of American cedar and deerskin.

In the 1930s, African Americans told government interviewers from the Works Progress Administration about using hand drums in their rituals. The drums may have been kept and played openly, or played illicitly and disassembled quickly when discovery threatened.

One place where we know African drumming continued unabated was at a location considered the seedbed of jazz, gospel, blues, and rock—Congo Square in New Orleans. Benjamin Latrobe, known as the "father of American architecture" and who worked in New Orleans, gives an eyewitness account from February 21, 1819 of encountering African American drummers playing on drums and other African instruments in Congo Square.

Rhythm Is Vital to Our Existence

Remember, the Little Drummer Boy brought his drumbeat to the baby Jesus as a gift (I bet Jesus smiled).

Rhythm is an important part of our physical existence. It manifests in our hearts and our breath. It exists in the ocean's tide, the changing of the seasons, the countdown of time on a clock, and the Earth's orbit. Rhythm exists in all of God's creations! Drumming is present in every culture. For centuries, people have used drumming in communication, music and dance, cultural events, rituals, ceremonies, healing, rites of passage, celebrations, and community building.

Rhythm manifests in our hearts and our breath

I have used drumming therapy with many groups of children and adults, not only to give them a break from the serious medical conditions many of them are fighting, but also to renew their sense of confidence and infuse them with refreshed energy through this invigorating experience.

In drumming therapy, we use the natural power of rhythm and music to enhance the healing process. Group drumming gets everyone in sync: it erases social barriers, encourages freedom of expression, and fosters unity. Drumming taps into people's dormant emotions and unexplainable feelings of excitement, peace, and ecstasy. It decreases depression, anxiety, and stress; boosts immune-system functioning, and improves physical health.

Reawakening your sense of symphonic mastery and accepting that you have great abilities are essential if you want to be enthusiastic about accomplishing your goals. Drumming can dramatically improve physiological, mental, and physical coordination, which makes it an extremely effective catalyst for learning and development.

Moving in rhythm is a primal reaction that is at the very core of our early development. A baby moves to the rhythm of music at a very early age. Who hasn't seen a cute baby bouncing and rocking to the beat of a song? It can be a crucial tool later, in the development of attentive listening, absorption, social, and comprehension skills. It appears that babies can recognize the pulse of a language as well as its pitch and melodic contour. This is an incredibly sophisticated ability. In addition to providing health and mood benefits, drumming can help us tap into, and express, our spiritual side. It is primal and powerful.

Terriea Harris, a women's outreach counselor who works with battered women, calls the drum "the heartbeat of Mother Earth." She writes, "Drum is a voice, a prayer to Spirit, is the voice of the Earth coming through to speak of its heart. Drumming connects us to our Creator, connecting our heart to the heartbeat of the Earth. It is a way to connect one's spirit with the Great Spirit."

"Bach gave us God's word. Mozart gave us God's laughter. Beethoven gave us God's fire. God gave us Music that we might pray without words."

—Inscription at the Alte Opera Haus in Frankfurt, Germany

Drumming: An Effective Team-Building Activity

In my Drumming Up Business consulting work, we use drum circles as a team-building activity. Drumming is an unexpected yet fun and stimulating activity that enhances many aspects of individual and group well-being. At a deep level, just about everyone recognizes basic drum patterns and the rhythms of African music. They have been the heartbeat of popular Western music for decades.

Getting in Tune

Paul Harvey once told this story on his popular radio show, about a sheepherder who had a violin, but couldn't play it because it was out of tune. He had no way to tune it, so in desperation he wrote to the radio station and asked them at a certain hour on a certain day if they would strike the note "A." The officials at the radio station decided they would accommodate the old fellow, and on that day the true tune of "A" was broadcast.

His fiddle was in tune, and once again his cabin echoed with joyful music. When we live apart from God our life gets out of harmony—with others and with God. At Drumming Up Business Edutainment Seminars, we are experienced in working with event planners to adapt the drum circle to suit the needs of your organization. There are many benefits to creating music in a group, and it is widely accepted by teachers, youth workers, music therapists, and health practitioners as being an effective way to encourage life skills and develop confidence and self-esteem.

When participants walk into the room where we conduct our drum circle, they see an impressive array of drums and percussion instruments. After a humorous warm-up, we facilitate simple interlocking activities that soon become musical and give everyone a palpable sense of achievement. The whole sound is powerful, resonant, and much greater than the sum of the parts—a great metaphor for a team.

Drum circles probably aren't the first type of team-building activity you consider for your organization. But I have witnessed significant transformations in the morale, camaraderie, and team spirit that result when leaders have their team members participate in drum circles. Here are just a few of the benefits your team and organization will experience:

- Academic development
- Camaraderie
- Confidence
- Cooperation
- Creativity
- Inclusion
- Motivational Learning
- Playfulness
- Respect
- Social Inclusion
- Teamwork
- Togetherness
- Unity

Individuals benefit from the interaction during drum circles, too. Participants get to express their creativity, develop their skills in social and emotional development, and enhance their musical and rhythmic understanding. Anyone can participate. Drum circles enhance these characteristics among individuals:

- Personal, social, and emotional skills
- Creativity, ingenuity, and quick thinking
- Awareness of self within the organization
- Cooperation vs. competition

- Personal integrity
- Creative thought process
- Emotional intelligence
- Leadership skills

Now, companies are using drum circles to improve team building and employee productivity. One barrier to corporate team building is that team members often see themselves as being in competition with one another. Drum circles can make teams more productive because the interaction makes the workplace more enjoyable.

Regardless of your age, gender, or background, drumming is an open door for everyone to try. When you plan your next family gathering or retreat, consider planning a drum circle as part of the event to bring the group together and open a new form of communication. Drumming is a great activity for senior groups, too. A study led by neurologist Barry Bittman of the Mind-Body Wellness Center in Meadville, Pennsylvania, found that patients who took part in group drumming, or drum circles, experienced increased levels of disease-fighting immune system cells called "natural killer cells." He attributed the change to the stress-reducing benefits of self-expression, camaraderie, and rhythmic drumming. (https://remo.com/experience/post/healthrhythms-benefits-of-participation/)

Not only do the right and left brain operate in different modes; they also usually operate in different brain-wave rhythms. The right brain may be generating alpha waves while the left brain is in a beta state, or both can be generating the same type of brain waves but remain out of sync with each other.

But in states of intense creativity, deep meditation, or under the influence of rhythmic sound, both left and right hemispheres may become entrained to the same rhythm. This state of unified whole-brain functioning is called "hemispheric synchronization" or "the awakened mind."

As the two hemispheres begin to resonate to a single rhythm, a sense of clarity and heightened awareness arises. The individual is able to draw on both the left and the right hemispheres simultaneously. The mind becomes sharper, more lucid, synthesizing much more rapidly than normal, and emotions are easier to understand and transform. The conscious and unconscious levels of the mind interface and integrate more easily. Insight quickens, and creative intuition flourishes, giving one the ability to visualize and bring into manifestation ideas more easily. Research has shown that playing rhythmic music is one of the most effective ways to induce brainwave synchronization.

Drumming Benefits Our Health

Music and drumming have been shown to reduce certain stress-causing hormones in the body, and they trigger the brain's pleasure-giving neurotransmitters, known as endorphins. When endorphins are released, they result in feelings of well-being and happiness. A healthy person is a happy person. From a physical-fitness viewpoint, drumming can be a catalyst for many types of physical exercise and coordination activities.

Drumming therapy taps into layers of the mind and body that other modalities cannot. Studies have shown that repetitive drumming changes brain-wave activity and induces a state of calm and focused awareness.

A 2016 study performed by researchers at the University of South Australia found that blasting rock music during chemotherapy treatments has been effective at "maximizing the efficiency of cancer drug delivery"—meaning, it helps get the drugs exactly where they need to go so that you stand a better chance of beating cancer or, at the very least, fighting your way into remission (Society of Rock 2020).

Drumming increases concentration and focus, helps develop communication skills, and encourages people to listen and communicate effectively with each other. It is a great way for people to explore their creativity, which leads to greater respect and understanding of themselves and others.

> *"Music is a higher revelation than all wisdom and philosophy."*
> **—Ludwig von Beethoven**

How Our Brains React to Drumming

The human brain is divided into two hemispheres that are basically split in their control of the thinking process. Typically, activity in the brain alternates between the left and right hemispheres.

The right side of the brain is generally more intuitive and visual. This is the creative or spontaneous side; many artists and musicians are right-brain-dominant. The left side of the brain is more logical and sequential in its way of processing thoughts. Many attorneys and scientists are left-brain-dominant. Balancing and developing both sides of the brain can facilitate learning, enhance creativity, and result in efficiency in our personal and professional lives.

These two parts of the brain play distinctly different roles in processing music, too. Layne Redmond, who died from cancer in 2013, was considered one of the world's foremost authorities on the small, hand-held frame drum, which women often played in the ancient Mediterranean world. She is the only woman who was named to *DRUM!* magazine's list of "Heavyweight Drummers Who Made a Difference in the '90s." Below, she explains how the two sides of the brain work in sync to process music:

The right brain functions as the creative, visual, aural, and emotional center. The left brain is the rational, logical, analytical, and verbal administrator. Generally, either the right or left brain dominates in cycles lasting from thirty minutes to three hours. While one hemisphere is dominant, the memories, skills, and information of the other hemisphere are far less available, residing in a subconscious or unconscious realm.

> **"Rhythm is the soul of life. The whole universe revolves in rhythm. Everything and every human action revolves in rhythm."**
> **—Babatunde Olatunji**

A *Scientific American* article reported that music can directly trigger physiological changes that modulate blood pressure, heart rate, and respiration. Researchers in one study noted that understanding the mechanisms of how swelling crescendos and deflating decrescendos affect our physiology could lead to potential new therapies for stroke and other conditions. The researchers found that changes in the cardiovascular and respiratory systems mirrored musical tempo (Peeples 2009).

Our bodies are packed with time-related systems. We have a built-in pulse, circadian rhythms, and great rhythmic awareness and ability. That's because we need a sense of rhythm to help cope with time-sensitive structures, sequences, and events. Timing is everything.

Drumming Affects Our Mood

In the 1930s, psychologist Kate Hevner Mueller discovered, through a series of experiments, "that tempo influence[s] our emotions more than any other characteristic." More than sixty years later, Lise Gagnon and Isabelle Peretz of the University of Montreal performed similar experiments. They reached the same conclusion: "The results confirm that both mode and tempo determine 'happy–sad' judgments in isolation, with the tempo being more salient, even when tempo salience was adjusted" (Madden 2014).

> *"Music can change the world because it can change people."*
>
> **—Bono**

Drummers Are Smarter Than Everyone Else!

Is there really any other member of the band that's as teased or shunned as the drummer? You've heard the age-old names drummers have been given over the years. "D.R.U.M. = Doesn't Really Understand Music" or "The only non-musician of the band." If you're a drummer, you're gonna get made fun of. However, that's all changing thanks to a little bit of scientific research!

Professor Frederic Ullen, from the Karolinska Institutet in Stockholm led a study to find out whether or not the ability to play drums/keep a beat could be linked to good problem-solving skills. In order to accomplish this, he and Guy Madison, from Sweden's Umea University, asked thirty-four right-handed men between the ages of nineteen and forty-nine to tap a drumstick at a variety of different intervals.

This study was done in quite a unique way and found that it's not just listening to music, but actually playing it that produces the higher threshold. Dunbar and his colleagues gathered twelve drummers who play together on a regular basis and nine musicians who worked at a musical instrument store and gave them a sixty-question intelligence test.

Frederic Ullen is quoted as saying, "We found that people with high general intelligence were also more stable on a very simple timing task. We also found that these participants had larger volumes of the white matter in the brain, which contains connections between brain regions" (Cleland 2008).

Researchers at the University of Oxford discovered that drummers produce a natural "high" when playing together, heightening both their happiness and their pain thresholds. They concluded that drum circles were the very foundation that made human society possible. As you can see, drumming is inherent in our nature and built into our physical makeup. Try drumming yourself. See how it can benefit you as an individual and also in groups you are a part of.

However, intelligence isn't the only perk you get from being a drummer. The University of Oxford led their own study and found that drummers typically have higher pain thresholds than people who are not drummers. The study was led by University of Oxford psychologist Robin Dunbar, who concluded that "people who have just been playing music have a higher tolerance for pain—an indication that their bodies are producing endorphins, which are sometimes referred to as natural opiates."

The drummers were asked to play together for thirty minutes straight, and the music store employees were asked to work their shifts for the same amount of time with music playing in the background. When the drummers finished playing and each employee was finished with their shift, they were given a pain threshold test. The drummers were able to tolerate significantly more of the painful stimulus before noting that they were in pain. "We conclude that it is the active performance of music that generates the endorphin high, not the music itself" (Jacobs 2017).

> *"A painter paints pictures on canvas. But musicians paint their music in silence."*
> **—Leopold Stokowski**

How Music Makes You Smarter

Have you ever noticed how your favorite music can make you feel better? Well, new research studies now show how music can make you smarter too! Scientists at Stanford University, in California, have recently revealed a molecular basis for the Mozart Effect, but not other music. Dr. Rauscher and her colleague H. Li, a geneticist, have discovered that rats, like humans, perform better on learning and memory tests after listening to a Mozart sonata (Singer 2004).

Science has now shown that our heartbeat tends to synchronize with the music, and thus we, in turn, relax and reach the alpha brainwave state. When we relax, the Reticular Activating Filter is open and therefore information flows straight through to memory, which is in the subconscious mind. That's why specially selected Baroque Music (with a timing of sixty beats per minute) is good for meditation, releasing stress, and accelerated learning techniques. Relaxation increases productivity.

Major corporations such as Shell, IBM, and Dupont, along with hundreds of schools and universities, use music, such as certain Baroque and Mozart Effect pieces, to cut learning time in half and increase retention of the new materials. According to the research outlined in the book, musical pieces, such as those of Mozart, can relieve stress, improve communication, and increase efficiency. Creativity scores soar when listening to Mozart.

"I think music in itself is healing. It's an explosive expression of humanity. It's something we are all touched by. No matter what culture we're from, everyone loves music."

—Billy Joel (Rolling Stone Magazine, Nov 6, 1986)

In my Drumming Up Business seminars, I have been using the Mozart Effect music for years as a strategy to reduce learning time and increase student memory of the material. Music activates the whole brain and makes you feel more energetic, and there is a well-documented link between music and learning.

Dr. Georgi Lozanov, the renowned Bulgarian psychologist, proved conclusively "that 'by using certain Baroque pieces, foreign languages can be mastered with 85-100 percent effectiveness in thirty days, when the usual time is two years.'" Students learning with Baroque Music were able to recall their second language with nearly 100 percent accuracy even after they had not studied it for four years (Shan 2014)!

For many years, with thousands of students, The Center for New Discoveries in Learning has been evaluating the use of music and learning both in the classroom and while students study. They have found that students using the Mozart Effect pieces and certain other Baroque pieces (recorded at about sixty beats per minute) felt calmer, could study longer, and had a higher rate of retention as well as earning better grades according to their teachers.

These special music Mozart Effect pieces, recorded at just the right tempo, activate the left and right brain for the maximum learning/retention effect. The music activates the right brain, and the words your child is reading or saying aloud activate the left brain. This increases the learning potential a minimum of five times according to the research.

When your body hears the one beat per second of music, your heart rate and pulse relax to the beat. When you are in this relaxed, but alert state, your mind is able to concentrate more easily. Music corresponds to and affects our physiological conditions.

Some of the benefits of the Mozart Effect are:

- Improves test scores
- Cuts learning time
- Calms hyperactive children and adults
- Reduces errors
- Improves creativity and clarity
- Heals the body faster
- Integrates both sides of the brain for more efficient learning
- Raises IQ scores nine points (Campbell 2001)

WALT DISNEY'S RULES FOR SUCCESS

Top 10 Drum Tips—How to Become the "One 2 Beat"

1. Show Some Magic

2. Invest in Knowledge

3. Diversify

4. Know Your Goals

5. Try It on a Small Scale First

6. Experiment

7. Help Your Community

8. Go with Your Feeling

9. Daydream

10. Have a Sense of Humor

Before we move on to Beat 10, let's review the strategies we learned in this chapter:

1.   Recognize the primal basis and the powerful impact that rhythm has on your body and everyday life.

2.   Consider hosting a drum circle in your group or organization to enhance camaraderie, team building, morale, and productivity.

3.   Try drumming yourself to improve your health, your mood— and even to become smarter than everyone else!

WIPEOUT
Crash and Burn

"When everything seems to be going against you, remember that the airplane takes off against the wind, not with it."
—Henry Ford

Are you experiencing wipeout in your life—a crash and burn?

According to the Urban Dictionary, here is one definition of "crash and burn": "to really screw up one's life by unforeseen circumstances or making bad choices (often accompanied by addictions in your life)" (*Urban Dictionary*, online edition, s.v. "crash and burn..").

At some point, we all face challenges—the loss of a job or a loved one, a broken marriage or relationship, an illness or medical emergency—that could easily bring us to the brink of despair. Negative thoughts can overpower you at such a time as this, bombarding your mind, telling you that you've seen your best days. Your future is bleak; your life is in ruins. Your future boils down to your expectations of what happens next. Pressure can make or break you. You can either make the best of the situation and move forward or wipe out—crash and burn.

When the US Marines are in harm's way or a dangerous place, they simply regroup, strategize, and then charge ahead. They respond to the threat. When faced with a negative circumstance, it's important that you don't have a knee-jerk reaction. Instead, respond to the situation with a clear plan of action. Adversity can bring out the best or worst in a person. Let it bring out the best in you. You're the "One 2 Beat." Take no prisoners. Failure is not an option.

> *"Whether you think you can or you think you can't, you're right."*
>
> **—Henry Ford**

Pay as little attention to discouragement as possible. Move full steam ahead like a ship, which moves forward whether facing rough or smooth seas, rain or shine. The goal is simply to make it to the port.

> *"When you get to the end of your rope, tie a knot in it and hang on."*
>
> **—Franklin D. Roosevelt**

Refuse to Let Circumstances Define You

Do crises which affect us or others in our homes, businesses, country, or elsewhere, seem to be crashing in on us? If so, we must put a stop to such distractions and get into such a living relationship with God that our relationship with others is maintained through the work of intercession, where God works His miracle.

In March of 2020, we experienced a pandemic virus that affected the world and caused death and economic shutdown like nothing the world has ever experienced.

"The winds of March are often cruel and blustery. And yet they typify the stormy seasons of my life. [We] should be glad to have the opportunity to come to know these seasons ... There is a certain glory of [God] that can only be seen when the wind is contrary and my ship is being tossed by the waves" (Cowman and Reiman 2001).

"You are on a long uphill journey and sometimes it seems endless to you. Looking back, you can see [the] times of ease and refreshment. Looking ahead, however, you see only a continuing ascent. The top of the mountain you are climbing is nowhere in sight. I know how hard it is for you to keep going day after day ... You live in a culture dedicated to entertainment and pleasure-seeking. In such a climate, a life struggle seems alien ... Try to view it, instead, as a rich opportunity: Your uphill journey keeps you aware of your neediness, so you look to [God] for help" (Young 2012).

"When God gives us an iron will, we can cut through difficulties just as an iron plowshare cuts through the hardest soil"
(Cowman and Reiman 2001).

It is possible to be highly knowledgeable and yet remain ignorant of the truth. Let me suggest four reasons why and how this is possible.

1. We are learning too much. Knowledge spells power and survival; we are continually packing our minds with new information. Spiritual truth is revealed to us in moments of quiet and unhurried reflection and contemplation.

2. We are learning the wrong "stuff." Much of what we learn lies outside the boundaries of God's intended knowledge for us, thus polluting the inner springs of our soul.

3. We are hindered in our learning by our pride, in our blinding arrogance.

4. Today, as you embark upon the challenges confronting you, keep in mind the Scriptural formula for experiencing God as your stronghold: "'My grace is sufficient for you, for my power is made perfect in weakness.' Therefore I will boast all the more

gladly about my weaknesses, so that Christ's power may rest on me" (2 Cor. 12:9).

"For when I am weak, then I am strong."
—2 Corinthians 12:10

People often experience wipeout, but instead of focusing on recovering from it, they wallow in their misery. You nurture a "victim mentality" — by refusing to take responsibility for your life. You believe, "no one appreciates you," "no one understands you," You say things like "I have had a tough life," "they have taken advantage of me," "I can't get out of this rut," "I've had too many negative circumstances." God's word says, "We are hard pressed on every side, but not crushed; perplexed but not in despair; persecuted, but not abandoned; struck down but not destroyed" (2 Cor. 4:8–9).

I do know what you're facing. I've had health issues—polio as a child and throat cancer just recently. You want to talk about poverty? I've been so broke in my life that I once had my car repossessed. An apartment complex tried to evict me once, and I had to take change to the bank to get a few dollars to buy food for my children. As for broken relationships, I went through a divorce. I was laid off after 9/11 because my job required international travel, and the company I worked for aborted all trips. I didn't know how I was going to take care of my children.

Sometimes heroism comes from scrambling to make it out of the abyss. This is the logic driving businesses that operate in highly uncertain environments, such as venture capital firms (whose success rates range from 10 to 20 percent), pharmaceutical companies (which typically create hundreds of new molecular entities before coming up with one marketable drug), and the movie business (where, according to one study, 1.3 percent of all films earn 80 percent of the box-office revenue).

Learn what doesn't work. Many successful ventures are built on failed projects. Apple's Macintosh computer emerged in part from the ashes of a now-forgotten product called Lisa, which introduced a number of the graphical user interfaces and mouse operations used in today's computers.

In truly uncertain situations, conventional market research is of little use. If you had asked people in 1990 what they would be willing to pay for an Internet search, no one would have known what you were talking about. A massive amount of experimentation was needed before workable search engines emerged. Early users sought to be paid for doing the searches.

Later, companies explored business models based on advertising. Later still, Google developed a system to maximize the profitability of the ad-based model. Without all that trial and error, it's highly unlikely that Google could have built the algorithm-based juggernaut that is so familiar today.

Create the conditions to attract resources and attention. Organizations tend to move on to new projects instead of fixing existing projects that have systemic problems. If something big goes wrong, though, it's all hands on deck!

You know, the smallest thing can change your life. In the blink of an eye, something happens by chance when you least expect it and sets you on a course you never planned … into a future you never imagined. Where will it take you? That's the journey of your life. You search for the light, but sometimes finding the light means you must pass through the deepest darkness. At least that's the way it was for me.

"Heroes aren't born, they're cornered."
—James Belushi

We are superheroes because of the joy that comes from experiencing the very things that look as if they are going to overwhelm us.

We lose interest and give up when we have no vision, no encouragement, and no improvement. Look past your immediate circumstances. They do not define you. In the long run, steady perseverance will push you to the finish line.

"I won't back down"

Use Failure to Your Advantage

Failure in life can provide valuable takeaways. A certain amount of failure can help you become stronger, more resilient, and wiser.

Keep your options open. As the range of possible outcomes for a course of action expands, the possibilities for success expand too. You'll improve your odds if you make more tries.

Balance Pressure and Rest

> *"People are like bicycles. They can keep their balance only as long as they keep moving."*
>
> **—Einstein**

Defy Obstacles, Like Michelangelo and Beethoven

Some of the most famous overachievers in the world rose above great adversity to thrive and excel. These fascinating people can teach us a thing or two about looking beyond our current circumstances.

Michelangelo

Michelangelo was an Italian sculptor, painter, architect, and poet. His works include the marble reliefs titled "Madonna of the Steps," "Battle of the Centaurs," the statue "David," and the frescoes of the Sistine Chapel. In the latter part of his life, he became involved in poetry and architecture. He helped design St. Peter's Basilica in Rome. He also worked for the Medici family and for popes, so he was able to enjoy his popularity while he was still alive, but Michelangelo had a rough start in life. His mother died when he was only six years old. He had a contentious personality and quick temper, which led to difficult relationships, often with his superiors. He sometimes fell into spells of melancholy, which were recorded in many of his literary works. He once wrote, "I am here in great distress and with great physical strain, and have no friends of any kind, nor do I want them; and I do not have enough time to eat as much as I need; my joy and my sorrow/my repose are these discomforts." In his youth, Michelangelo had taunted a fellow student and received a blow to his nose that disfigured him for life.

Despite his troubles, he strived to be a good man and a good artist. He overcame adversity every way he knew. He is widely regarded as the most famous artist of the Italian Renaissance. Like all of us, Michelangelo had shortcomings, and some of them could have ruined his future. But he was destined to be an artist. He nurtured his God-given talent and succeeded. If he had given in to the adversity he faced, he would never have achieved notoriety and worldwide acclaim.

> *"Every adversity, every failure, every heartache carries with it the seed of an equal or greater benefit."*
> **—Napoleon Hill**

Beethoven

This theme of the 1931 classic self-help book *Think and Grow Rich* by Napoleon Hill can hardly be better expressed in musical history than by the life and music of Ludwig van Beethoven. For most of his adult life, Beethoven suffered the greatest adversity possible for a musician and composer: deafness. Yet somehow, he found the "seed" in that problem that enabled him to compose some of the greatest and most moving pieces of music in the history of humanity.

He is one of the most well-known composers of all time. Most people, young or old, know the name Beethoven even if they know of no other composer. Beethoven was the last and greatest of the classical period of composers. And the intensity, emotional depth, and individual expression of his work launched the Romantic period. The last movement of his ninth symphony was chosen as the official hymn of the United Nations. More importantly, it remains the greatest expression of joy. It sounds as though God gave Beethoven a glimpse of the wonder of heaven (Biography.com 2020).

Life is like a piano. The white keys represent happiness, and the black keys show sadness. But the black keys also make music. Without them, music played on the piano would be incomplete. As you journey through life, recognize the value of sorrow and times of darkness. "In some realms of nature, shadows are the places of greatest growth. The beautiful Indian corn never grows more rapidly than in the darkness of a warm summer night … Lands with fog, clouds, and shade are lush with greenery. And there are some beautiful flowers that bloom in shade that will never bloom in sunlight" (Cowman 2016). Diamonds are made from coal that is put under extreme pressure.

> The beauties of nature often emerge after the storm. The rugged beauty of the mountain is born in a storm, and the heroes of life are the storm-swept and battle-scarred. You have been in the storms and swept by the raging winds? Have they left you broken, weary, and beaten in the valley, or have they lifted you to the sunlit summits of a richer, deeper, more abiding manhood or womanhood? Have they left you with more sympathy for the storm-swept and the battle-scarred? (Cowman 2016)

Dwight Hill, the author of a blog called "Net Profits," wrote the following,

> One of the toughest battles that you'll face in your life is with yourself:
>
> "Your self-incrimination from an over-active conscience. Your fear of rejection ... failure ... the future. Your inner spiritual turmoil over re-appearing sin."
>
> Many people succumb in their lives to the same aimless, native blandness: putting out fires. Solving problems. Oiling the wheel that squeaks the loudest. Oppressive ... ... boring ... survival (Hill 1995).

"If all of life were sunshine, our face would long to gain
And feel once more upon it, the cooling splash of rain."
—Henry Jackson Van Dyke

We are super-victors with a joy that comes from experiencing the very things that look as if they are going to overwhelm us. A piano adjusts to the tension of its strings, which generally amounts to 38,000 pounds of pressure. Without that tension, that pressure, the piano would not be in tune or play beautiful music. The same can be true in our lives, too. Many newspaper reporters admit that the pressure of a deadline energizes them into action. And competition gets the adrenaline flowing, whether it's a debating championship or an Olympic relay. We sometimes need pressure to propel our lives forward.

If we would only move straight ahead in faith, the path would be open for us. But sometimes we stand still, waiting for the obstacles to be removed, when we should go forward as if there were no obstacles at all (Cowman). Just as we need pressure, we also need rest. There is no music during a musical rest, but the rest is needed to make music. In the melody of our lives, the music is separated here and there by rests. If we are under pressure all the time, we can burn out. We can wipe out. Crash and burn. It's important to balance the pressure with the rest. Both are necessary for us to make progress.

> *"Huge waves that would frighten an ordinary swimmer can produce a tremendous thrill for the surfer who has ridden them."*
> **—Oswald Chambers**

When Necessity Calls, "Drum Up Biscuits"

In 1991, I was working for a laser tag entertainment franchise called Q-Zar, which was owned by U2. I was living the high life, so to speak. I moved to Dallas, Texas, and was making tons of money and having a ball. I was buying everything I could possibly want, from houses to new cars, and sending my children to private school. But in 1997, it was "game over." Q-Zar dispersed and was going out of business. I found myself once again without a job. My family had a routine. We would go to church every Sunday and then have lunch at Spring Creek, the greatest five-star buffet. It was very expensive, but it was certainly a treat for my family and me. They had the tastiest peach cobbler. All their food was outstanding, but my kids loved the hot biscuits best.

When I lost my job, I had just enough money in the bank to keep paying the bills, but we couldn't afford to go to fancy restaurants like that anymore. One Sunday after church, my kids, who were about five years old and ten years old at the time, asked if we could go to Spring Creek. I said, "Kids, I've got a better idea—a special treat that you're just going to love."

I looked over at my wife, and she had a blank stare on her face, as if asking, "What are we going to do?" She knew I probably had less than five dollars in my pocket at the time. I started driving and pulled into Kentucky Fried Chicken. They all stayed in the car as I went in. Moments later, I came out with a big box and brought it into the car. The aroma was wonderful. When I opened the corner of the box, the steam escaped, and I unveiled what was inside the box: succulent hot biscuits with melted butter all over them.

My son said, "Daddy, can I have two?"

My daughter repeated, "Daddy, can I have two, too?"

"Of course," I said. "Have as many as you like."

My son said, "Mommy, isn't Daddy the best? He always comes up with the bestest ideas!"

I looked over at my wife and saw tears coming down her face. I thought, "Heroes are not born; they're cornered." I was cornered. I needed to feed my children, and I wanted to make it fun and exciting for them. I call this "drumming up biscuits."

If you are facing a situation you've never encountered before, think differently than you have in the past. The solutions you employed for past problems probably won't solve your new problems. It's uncharted territory. The old saying goes, "Necessity is the mother of invention." Just think—if it weren't for dire circumstances, many inventions would have never been created. "Drum up biscuits" when you are backed into a corner.

The Cinderella Man—Believe in the Fairy-Tale Ending ...

I can remember the emotional pain of going through a divorce. I moved from New York to Orlando with my children and was faced with raising my two children on my own. One day, my daughter looked up at me and asked, "Daddy, are we going to be all right?"

I said, "Are you kidding? We are going to be fantastic. We're going to have a great life."

But inside, I was thinking, "*Oh my God, what am I going to do now?*" I had no option … my children were counting on me, and I wasn't going to let them down. One of my favorite movies was *Cinderella Man*, an American film by Ron Howard, titled after the nickname of heavyweight boxing champion James J. Braddock and inspired by his life story during the Great Depression. My birthday was in the following month, and my kids bought me a shadow box with Everlast Boxing Gloves in it and a caption that read, "Bob DelVecchio, The Cinderella Man." I cried tears of joy. It is probably the best gift I ever received.

Focus on What You Have

When I was a young child, we didn't have much money, so our food choices were limited, to say the least. One day, my dad decided to make dinner. The only thing we had was kidney beans, sauce, and bread. He cooked the sauce with the beans and put chunks of bread in it. We couldn't get enough of it. It was delicious! I asked him what it was called, and he said, "Poor Man's Stew—fit for a king!"

As we grew older and our financial situation improved, I remember my mother asking us if we wanted steak and potatoes for dinner. We said, "No! Can Dad make our favorite—Poor Man's Stew?" What a memory of a happy moment in our lives. The point here is to focus on what you have instead of on what you don't have. You might just invent something great. It comes down to, "What are you going to do with what you got."

"It's not where you're from; it's where you're going.
It's not what you drive; it's what drives you.
It's not what's on you; it's what's in you.
It's not what you think; it's what you know."
—A Gatorade commercial

Fail by Design

It's hardly news that business leaders work in increasingly uncertain environments. Nor will it surprise anyone that under uncertain conditions, failures are more common than successes. Yet, strangely, we don't design organizations to manage, mitigate, and learn from failures.

When I ask executives how effective their organizations are at learning from failure, on a scale of one to ten, I often get a sheepish, "Two—or maybe three" in response. As this suggests, most organizations are profoundly biased against failure and make no systematic effort to study it. Executives hide mistakes or pretend they were always part of the master plan. Failures become taboo subjects, not to be discussed. People grow so afraid of hurting their career prospects by making a mistake that they eventually stop taking risks. I'm not going to argue that failure is a good thing. Far from it—it can waste money, destroy morale, infuriate customers, damage reputations, harm careers, and sometimes lead to tragedy. Failure is inevitable in uncertain environments; but, if managed well, it can be a very *useful* thing. Indeed, organizations can't possibly undertake the risks necessary for innovation and growth if they're not comfortable with the idea of failing.

This is true in our personal lives, too. Everyone makes mistakes; it's not realistic to think you can skate through life without making any. Don't be so hard on yourself—good can come out of your mistakes. Your finite mind tends to look backward, longing to undo decisions you've come to regret. This is a waste of time and energy, leading only to frustration. Instead of floundering in the past, move on from your mistakes; because you are human, you will continue to make mistakes. Thinking that you should live an error-free life is symbolic of pride. Your failures can be a source of blessing. They humble you and give you empathy for other people's struggles and weaknesses.

An alternative to ignoring failure is to foster "intelligent failure," a phrase coined by Duke University's Sim Sitkin in a terrific 1992 *Research in Organizational Behavior* article titled "Learning Through Failure: The Strategy of Small Losses." If your organization can adopt the concept of intelligent failure, it will become more agile, better at risk taking, and more adept at organizational learning. (Sitkin 1992)

Winston Churchill, who suffered many setbacks in life said, "Success is going from failure to failure with no loss of enthusiasm."

Although Churchill was born into British aristocracy, he did poorly in school and failed the entrance exam for the Royal Military College three times before being admitted. He was accident-prone as a kid and suffered several serious injuries. When he served as First Lord of the Admiralty, he launched an amphibious assault during World War I against the crumbling Ottoman Empire in March 1915. But Ottoman troops sank three of their ships, severely damaged three others, and sent the remainder into retreat. Allied troops suffered more than 250,000 casualties in the process. Churchill lost his admiralty post as a result of the failure, although he was eventually able to restore his reputation. Twenty years later he was voted out of office before World War II ended.

William Manchester was a Professor of History Emeritus at Wesleyan University who wrote a bestselling book titled *The Last Lion*, a multi-volume biography of Winston Churchill. He noted that Churchill "understood the inevitability of setbacks when pursuing a bright triumph ... what set him apart was his incredible grit. To Churchill, anything was possible. Victory was always at hand." He once advised students at Harrow School, "Never give in! Never, never, never, never!" (Greenspan 2014).

People like Churchill refuse to equate the occasional setback with defeat. They expect some dry spells along the way to their successful outcomes. Let's face it—dark hours are inevitable, and we can learn from them. Expect some dry spells, and move on.

> *"Don't ask yourself what the world needs.*
> *Ask what makes you come alive, and go do it*
> *because what the world needs is people who*
> *have come alive."*
> **—Howard Thurman**

It's really about focusing less on what other people think is important and more on what you were actually created to accomplish. Is the midnight closing 'round you? Are you facing difficult times? God allows us to go through tough times for our refinement and His glory. God has a plan for us, and we are assured of a great future if we choose to obey Him.

Grow through Setbacks

Trials in difficult times are needed to press us forward. They work in the way the fire in the furnace of the mighty steamship provides the energy that moves the pistons, turns the engine, and propels the great vessel across the sea, even when facing the wind and the waves. The person who may appear to be blessed, having been untouched by sorrow, is typically not one who is strong and at peace. His or her qualities have never been tested, and he or she does not know how they would handle even a mild setback.

A women's ministry called The Barry Ministry wrote about the value of conflict:

It may seem paradoxical, but the only person who is at rest has achieved peace through conflict. Conflict is not the ominous lull before the storm; instead, it's serenity in the quietness following the storm, with its fresh, purified air. The result of getting through conflict is confidence, safety, and peace. (http://thebarryagency.com/Christian/Womens%20 Ministries%20Articles/2009_Feb_Newsletter.htm

It has been said that a little bird will never sing the song its owner desires to hear as long as its cage is full of light. Many people are the same; they never learn to sing until the shadows of darkness fall upon them. It is a real and unquestionable fact of human life and culture that a person's character and strength become strongest during the darkest days.

The trials we go through either make us sweeter, better, and nobler men and woman, or they make us more critical, more fault finding, and more insistent on getting our own way. The things that happen either make us more evil or they make us more saintly, depending entirely on our relationship with God and our level of intimacy.

One of the toughest battles you will continually face in life is with yourself. When life takes unexpected turns, and things don't turn out as you had hoped, you can complain about your bad luck, or you can choose to win *despite* your circumstances. Only through pain can you achieve greatness.

My daughter, Daira DelVecchio, celebrated her thirty-second birthday, only to have the festivities cut short by a single phone call; her life-long best friend had just died. What a devastating blow this was to her, as she cried and tried to explain to me in a broken-down voice … "Alex is gone." I cried with her (Alex was like a second daughter to me), as I tried to comfort my daughter from the pain she was feeling. Here is a note of encouragement that she posted on Facebook to help others experiencing the pain of losing a loved one:

I believe that you cannot fully embrace JOY until you have also experienced the depths of PAIN and seen God's faithfulness in the deepest of your valleys.

Today is proving to be a challenging day of writing at my local coffee shop. I thought a "public" place would prevent me from having a "sob-fest" but … I was wrong.

As many of you know, a month ago I found myself celebrating my birthday in Nashville, TN with only one "wish"—to finish a yearlong project, a book I have been writing on JOY.

The second day into editing, I received the news that my best friend in the entire world, my sister had passed away. It felt like a tornado had blown right through my life, a whirlwind of wreckage and I was left in absolute rubble. Yet, knowing that God doesn't leave us brokenhearted, I was determined to pick my heart up off of the ground— even if shattered in pieces—and hand it over to Him.

Knowing it has been almost a month since my life changed forever, I decided today to finish the final chapter I had been avoiding writing on—Surviving Our Pain. The Bible says that when we experience trials, we have the ability to come out of them as gold— just like an ugly rock undergoing tremendous heat to produce something beautiful underneath the layers of impurities.

I know God is faithful and, in the middle of our deepest pain, only He can produce gold in our lives. Because I have always known this to be true and I am currently experiencing it little by little, day by day, I knew it was time to write on it.

I must say God is giving me words I didn't even know were buried within me. However, I am also writing this through SO many tears that my cheeks feel hot from all the emotion I didn't want to have to feel again—as if telling this story in pain, my story, would reawaken every moment of what can only be considered as the worst day of my life.

Courage for me today looks like choosing to share my pain, to ultimately help someone else find joy that they didn't think could be theirs to hold onto. It's a day of hope even if the tears might look otherwise. So, I keep on keeping on—because I truly believe that you cannot fully embrace joy until you have also experienced the depths of pain and seen God's faithfulness in the deepest of your valleys. I want to live this out every day, not just preach it half-heartedly. I guess that means today I have to do just that … really live it.

The world is full of hurting and comfortless hearts. But before you will be competent for this lofty ministry, you must be trained. And your training is extremely costly, to make it complete, you too must endure the same afflictions that are wringing countless hearts of tears and blood. Consequently, your own life becomes the hospital ward where you are taught the divine art of comfort. You will be wounded so that in the binding up of your wounds by the Great Physician, you may learn how to render first aid to the wounded everywhere.

Do you wonder why you're having to experience some great sorrow? Over the next ten years, you will find many others afflicted in the same way. You will tell them how you suffered and were comforted. As the story unfolds, God will supply the anesthetic.

> *"What lies behind you and what lies in front of you, pales in comparison to what lies inside of you."*
> **—Ralph Waldo Emerson**

Replace Fear with Faith

Fear is the opposite of faith, and it's displeasing to God. Fear clouds our judgment, paralyzes our actions, and causes us to delay our decisions and rationalize bad decisions. Fear promotes paranoia, induces us to think irrationally, destroys our trust in others, and diminishes our ability to believe. Fear is often a by-product of our pride. It can cause us to refuse to believe that God is in control. Fear diminishes our ability to drum up business.

Fear is the opposite of faith

> *"Don't be afraid, Jim. [Captain Kirk] The unknown is for us to conquer, not fear."*
> **—Mr. Spock**

How do we break the bondage of the cycle of fear? By choosing to believe God and act on His promises. "God has not given us a spirit of fear, but of power and of love and of a sound mind." 2 Tim.1:7 (NKJV) You and I have a simple choice to make: either we allow the demons of fear, doubt, and inadequacy to paralyze and diminish us to spiritual midgets, or we rise above our circumstances and claim God's promises.

You may be alone, but you never have to be lonely! God is with you! Reach for Him. People may have overlooked and forgotten you, but God has not! He will reward you for all that you have done! You can't walk on water if you don't get out of the boat. So conquer your fear, and push forward (Ortberg 2001).

> *"The ultimate measure of a man is not where he stands in moments of comfort and convenience, but where he stands at times of challenge and controversy."*
> —**Martin Luther King, Jr.**

The following was reportedly written years ago by a young Pastor in Africa. It was found tacked to the wall of his home after he was martyred.

"My Commitment as a Christian"

I'm part of a fellowship of the unashamed. I have the Holy Spirit power. The die has been cast. I have stepped over the line.

The decision has been made. I'm a disciple of Jesus. I won't look back, let up, slow down, back away, or be still.

My past is redeemed, my present makes sense, my future is secure.

I'm finished and done with low living, sight walking, small planning, smooth knees, colorless dreams, tamed visions, mundane talking, cheap giving, dwarfed goals.

I no longer need pre-eminence, prosperity, position, promotions, plaudits or popularity. I don't have to be right, first, tops, recognized, praised, regarded, or rewarded. I now live by faith, lean on his presence, walk by patience, live by prayer, and labor by power.

I won't give up, shut up, let up, until I have stayed up, stored up, prayed up, and preached up for the cause of Christ. I am a disciple of Jesus. I must go till He comes, give till I drop, preach all I know, and work till He stops me. And when He comes for His own, He will have no problem recognizing me. My banner will be clear.

Zion, hear me! It is true what many of you have heard. The machines have gathered an army and as I speak that army is drawing nearer to our home. Believe me when I say we have a difficult time ahead of us. But if we are to be prepared for it, we must first shed our fear of it. I stand here, before you here now, truthfully unafraid. Why?– Because I believe something you do not? No! I stand here without fear because I remember. I remember that I am here not because of the path that lies before me, but because of the path that lies behind me. I remember that for one hundred years we have fought these machines. I remember that for one hundred years they have sent their armies to destroy us and after a century of war I remember that which matters most! We are still here! Today, let us send a message to that army. Tonight, let us shake this cave. Tonight, let us tremble these walls of earth, steel, and stone, let us be heard from red core to black sky! Tonight let us make them remember, this is Zion, and we are not afraid!

—**Morpheus in *The Matrix Reloaded* (2003) movie**

ROBERT KIYOSAKI'S
RULES FOR SUCCESS

Top 10 Drum Tips—How to Become the "One 2 Beat"

1. Experience Makes You Smarter

2. The More You Give, the More You Receive

3. Change the Way You Think

4. Focus

5. Hard Times Bring New Opportunities

6. Design Business Properly

7. Know What You Are Working Hard For

8. Don't Be Afraid of Losses

9. Aim to Acquire Assets

10. Stop Saving Money, Hedge It

Before we move on to Beat 11, let's review the strategies covered in this chapter:

1. Refuse to let circumstances define you.

2. Use failure to your advantage.

3. Defy obstacles, as did Michelangelo and Beethoven.

4. Balance pressure and rest.

5. When necessity calls, "drum up biscuits" (improvise!).

6. Believe in the fairy-tale ending, like Cinderella.

7. Focus on what you have.

8. Fail by design.

9. Expect some dry spells.

10. Grow through setbacks.

11. Replace fear with faith.

BEATING THE ODDS
How to Recover

*"Let me tell you something you already
know. The world ain't all sunshine and
rainbows. It's a very mean and nasty place. I
don't care how tough you are, the world will
beat you to your knees and keep you there
permanently if you let it. Nobody is gonna
hit as hard as life. But it ain't about how hard
you're hit. It's about how hard you can get
hit and keep moving forward That's how
winning is done!"*
—Rocky Balboa in *Rocky*

Archie Moore was an American Light Heavyweight World Champion
Boxer from 1952 to 1962. He had one of the longest professional careers
in the history of the sport. When asked, "What did you think when you
were knocked down?" He said, "I don't belong here. I'm the champion."

Boxing is a good analogy for leadership development because it's
all about daily preparation. Even if a person has a natural talent, he or
she has to prepare and train to become successful. And when you get
knocked down, you've got to get back up if you want to win.

One of President Theodore Roosevelt's most famous quotes about
perseverance uses a boxing analogy: "It is not the critic who counts; not
the man who points out how the strong man stumbles, or where the

doer of deeds could have done them better. The credit belongs to the man who is actually in the arena, whose face is marred by dust and sweat and blood; who strives valiantly; who errs, who comes short again and again … who knows great enthusiasms, the great devotions; who spends himself in a worthy cause … "

> **"Every champion was once a contender who refused to give up."**
>
> **—Rocky**

Those who know me well, know the heart I have for children beating cancer and my passion for Drumming Up Business to help others achieve success in life. Don't we sometimes wonder why we go through such trials and tribulations? My bout with cancer has made me ponder this question. Then God revealed the answer … This gave me the peace that surpasses all understanding: God's ways are not our ways, as we learn from Isaiah. 55:8. " 'For my thoughts are not your thoughts, neither are your ways my ways,' declares the LORD."

Don't be fooled by the way things appear at a given moment in time. You are looking at only a very small piece of a massively big picture. From your limited perspective, your journey may be confusing, with puzzling twist and turns. "However, from my limitless, big-picture perspective. I am indeed leading you along straight." (Young 2012).

> **"Only a man who knows what it is like to be defeated can reach down to the bottom of his soul and come up with the extra ounce of power it takes to win when the match is even."**
>
> **—Muhammad Ali**

Use Hope to Overcome Hardship

"Little faith will bring your soul to heaven; but great faith will bring heaven to your soul."

—Charles H. Spurgeon

While I was in the middle of "beating" cancer, Pastor Paula (Paula White, a senior pastor at New Destiny Christian Center, a megachurch in Apopka, Florida) told me:

> I see a ministry that you have. You will speak to all nations. I've met millions of people around the world. You're special. I have a strong spiritual connection to you. With freedom comes boldness and a courageous attitude. Your test is your testimony. God has divine appointments, purpose, and destiny for you. You will be a world changer and a history maker!

That powerful message from a woman of God gave me hope. One of the greatest gifts leaders can give to those around them is hope. Never underestimate its power. A reporter once asked Winston Churchill what his country's greatest weapon was against Hitler's Nazi regime. Pausing, Churchill said, "It was what anyone's greatest weapon always has been: hope."

Hope is a powerful tool that can make you a boxer who wins outside the ring!

"The fight is won or lost far away from witnesses— behind the lines, in the gym and out there on the road, long before I dance under those lights."

—Muhammad Ali

Don't be afraid to fight to be a world changer. Hurting people hurt other people. If you don't know how to encourage yourself, you'll never be able to help anyone else. Give it over to God. There is hope in the knowledge that He is more powerful than we could ever hope to be.

Be kind because everyone is fighting a battle. People will push forward through difficult times if they have hope. Hope lifts people's morale. It improves our attitude and self-image. It reenergizes us. It raises our expectations. Maintaining hope comes from seeing the potential in every situation and staying positive, despite our circumstances. I want you to view trials as exercises designed to develop your trust muscle. Faith is what will get you there.

> *"Hope walks through the fire and faith leaps over it."*
>
> **—Jim Carrey**

Let Go of the Need to Control

According to a research team headed by Chapman University in Orange, California, the following are Americans' most pressing fears and concerns:

- Corruption of government officials
- Terrorist attacks
- Not having enough money for the future
- Being a victim of terror
- Government restrictions on firearms and ammunition
- Loved ones dying
- Economic or financial collapse
- Identity theft
- Loved ones becoming seriously ill
- Affordable health care

—*The Voice*, October 21, 2020

We could spend all day and all night worrying about these situations. But that won't get us anywhere except discouraged. We can't control these situations, but God can.

What happens when we cannot call the shots, control circumstances, or determine the outcome of a situation? Are our peace of mind and our sense of worth so fragile that they are predicated on the guarantee of life's optimum circumstances or upon a continual stream of successes and recognition? When we let go of the need to control and let God take on that responsibility, it frees up our energy and focus so that we can concentrate on achieving our goals. God is in control of the situation. God allows us to go through tough times for our refinement and His glory. God has a plan for us. God assures us of a great future if we choose to obey Him. God is faithful, and He will not let you be tempted beyond your ability.

> *"God is faithful; he will not let you be tempted beyond what you can bear. But when you are tempted, he will also provide a way out so that you can endure it."*
> **—1 Corinthians 10:13**

As I listened and slowly learned to obey God, His "gentle whisper" became for me the voice of prayer, wisdom, and service. No longer did I need to work so hard to think, pray, or trust because the Holy Spirit's "gentle whisper" quieted my heart, so I could hear God's voice in the secret places of my soul. It was His answer to all my questions. His strength permeated my soul and body. His voice became the essence of all knowledge, prayer, and blessings, for it was the living God Himself speaking to me.

*Do not pray for easy lives; pray to be a
stronger person.
Do not pray for tasks equal to your powers.
Pray for powers equal to your tasks.
Then the doing of your work will be no
miracle, but you shall be the miracle."*
—Phillips Brooks

Focus and Persevere to Accomplish Your Mission

Our trials are great opportunities, but too often we simply see them as obstacles. If only we would recognize that God has chosen to prove His love to us through difficult situations, those obstacles would then become evidence of God's infinite power. If we would look at our past, most of us would realize that during the times we endured great distress and felt that every path was blocked, our Heavenly Father chose to do the kindest things for us and bestow His richest blessings on us.

"Be men of courage; be strong."
—1 Corinthians 16:13

So much craziness going on around us today—wars, conflicts, persecution, violence, crime, natural disasters, terrorism, economic uncertainty, unemployment, divisions, disease, death. We fear for our children's future, we fear for our families, we fear for our financial future, we fear for our safety. The list goes on and on. There actually is a lot we could potentially worry about.

I read words of life and of truth. Soaking them in, over and over, praying them out loud. Until they became so familiar, they replace the other things in my mind that I'd battle against. There's nothing magical about words and verses, but there is power through them because they're God's words.

His words are "life" words, soothing to our soul, calming to our spirits, giving power to our days.

Do you believe you can accomplish your mission? Or are you paralyzed by indecision and analysis paralysis? Do you have the courage to believe that failure is not an option and that you will circumvent, tunnel through, or soar above the obstacles until your mission is accomplished?

Some people go after what they want with great enthusiasm and focus, while others just mosey along, hoping inspiration strikes them. The difference between eagles and chickens is a good illustration for this concept. Eagles soar with the wind, rising above their circumstances to see the big picture. Once they spot their prey, they drop down with lighting speed to accomplish their mission of capturing a fresh meal. Chickens cluck, peck, strut, mill around, and lay eggs when the urge comes upon them. Which are you? An eagle, who rises above his circumstances, combining vision, faith, and courage with coordinated effort, or are you a business-as-usual chicken that struts around and clucks, performing only when the urge comes upon you?

When you're going through an adverse situation, tormented, anxious, sad, fearful, depressed, stressed, and a mess, write down ten things for which you are grateful. It will eradicate your anxiety. It works like a miracle, I promise you!

> *"The tears you shed water the seeds that manifests victory in your life."*
> **Bobby DelVecchio**

Albert Einstein said, "Anyone who has never made a mistake has never tried anything new." If we look at the most prolific inventors throughout history, they failed many times—but they kept trying. Consider these famous people who refused to give up:

- Thomas Edison had thousands of failures before he got the light bulb right.

- Benjamin Franklin, the fool on the roof who flew his kite in a rainstorm, retired as one of our country's first millionaires.

- Albert Einstein wasn't able to speak until he was almost four years old, and his teachers said he would "never amount to much."

- Walt Disney was fired from a newspaper for "lacking imagination" and "having no original ideas."

- Oprah Winfrey was demoted from her job as a news anchor because she "wasn't fit for television."

- Michael Jordan, after being cut from his high school basketball team, locked himself in his room and cried.

- Steve Jobs, at thirty years old, was left devastated and depressed after unceremoniously being removed from the company he started.

- The Beatles were rejected by Decca Recording Studios, who said, "We don't like their sound. They have no future in show business."

"Circumstances don't make the man; they only reveal him to himself."
— **Epictetus**

Appreciate the Hardships That Make You Stronger

Easy, worry-free living that is free of challenges isn't what builds character. Suffering is what builds character. If we never have to overcome hardships and setbacks, we will never grow. Think about situations in your life that were difficult. It took a lot of courage, innovation, and perseverance to get through them, right? As you overcome those difficulties, you grow and become wiser. The trials of life are presented to make us, not break us. Financial troubles may destroy a person's business and build up his character. A direct blow may be the greatest blessing possible today for a person. If God places or allows anything difficult in our lives, we can be sure the real danger or trouble will be what we lose if we rebel against it (paraphrased from Maltbie D. Babcock).

> *Heroes are forged on anvils hot with pain,*
> *And splendid courage comes but with the test.*
> *Some natures ripen and some natures bloom*
> *Only on blood-wet soil; some souls prove great*
> *Only in moments dark with death or doom.*
> **—Ella Wheeler Wilcox**

God finds his best soldiers on the mountains of affliction (paraphrased from Charles Spurgeon).

> *"We can't solve problems by using the same kind of thinking we used when we created them."*
> **—Albert Einstein**

I am the captain of my ship, the master of my fate and God is my compass. Some people always avoid things that are costly or that require self-denial, self-restraint, and self-sacrifice. Yet it's hard work and difficulties that ultimately lead us to greatness.

Power, intelligence, athletic ability, efficiency, and affluence are among the values we highly esteem and sometimes idolize in other people. But we frown on human frailty, weakness, and poverty. In our society, there is little tolerance for those who are second or third string. And there isn't much respect among us for older people. They're out of touch, slow, not cool. Not "with it."

The pressure of difficult times adds value to life. Every time we emerge from some sort of trial, it's like a new beginning. We better understand the value of that trial. As a result, we apply ourselves more effectively for God and humankind. And the pressure we endure helps us understand the trials of others, equipping us to help them and sympathize with them. Trials in difficult times actually help us move forward.

> *"In times of great stress or adversity, it's always best to keep busy, to plow your anger and your energy into something positive."*
>
> **—Lee Iacocca**

The best response to adversity is a heart overflowing with gratitude. God is training you to cultivate a faithful mindset. This is like building your house on a firm rock—life's storms cannot shake you. As you learn these lessons, you are to teach them to others. He will open the way before you, one step at a time. Each of us sometimes has to walk through this world wearing a bright smile while our hearts are breaking. But to beat the odds, we need to keep a positive attitude (the "good foot") as we endure painful and distressing experiences. As you do, it will be of great use to others. When we persevere until the fight is over, we gain wisdom, deepen our peace, increase our courage, and amplify our power.

It may seem paradoxical, but the person who is at rest has achieved that serenity through conflict. This peace born of conflict is not like the ominous lull before the storm, but like the serenity in the quietness following the storm, with its fresh, purified air. The final result is confidence, safety, and peace. Rejoice when you face a wipeout. Appreciate not what is happening *to* you but what is about to happen *for* you.

> *"Today is my day to paint in bold colors, set today's rhythm with my heart-drum, walk today's march with courage, create today as my celebration of life."*
> **—Jonathan Lockwood Huie**

Ever get in a slump and can't get excited about drumming up business? Or even drumming up enthusiasm for your daily routine? This is often due to lack of motivation or stimulation. Find ways to get excited about life. The best response to adversity is a heart overflowing with gratitude.

> *"Count your blessings. Once you realize how valuable you are and how much you have going for you, the smiles will return, the sun will break out, the music will play, and you will finally be able to move forward the life that God intended for you with grace, strength, courage, and confidence."*
> **—Og Mandino**

TONY ROBBINS'S RULES FOR SUCCESS

Top 10 Drum Tips—How to Become the "One 2 Beat"

1. Raise Your Standards

2. Be Truly Fulfilled

3. Progress Equals Happiness

4. Love Your Customers

5. Add Value

6. Have an Exit Strategy

7. Be Resourceful

8. Pay Attention to the Little Things

9. Look for Leverage

10. Change Your Mindset

Before we move on to Beat 12, let's review the strategies we learned in this chapter:

1. Use hope to overcome hardship.

2. Let go of the need to control.

3. Focus and persevere to accomplish your mission.

4. Appreciate the hardships that make you stronger.

5. Get motivation from external sources.

BEAT
12

"ROLL" MODELS
Your Mentors

"Walk with the wise and become wise,
for a companion of fools suffers harm."
—Proverbs 13:20 (NIVUK)

No, that's not a typo in the chapter title. This chapter is about "role models," or people we look up to. I spelled it "roll models" to capture the spirit of a drum roll. It is well known that role models can change our lives, both by example and through teaching. We intentionally or unconsciously try to follow our role models' behavior, even though we are no doubt very different from our heroes. It is helpful to choose role models who have personalities similar to ours, but that's not always possible.

"The rhythm is gonna get you … " When I was growing up, my biggest "roll" model was Buddy Rich. Wow! What a drummer. I was mesmerized by his quick hands, precision playing, and dedication to perfection as a drummer. The second part of my life, my mother, Gina Marie DelVecchio-Handy, was my mentor and best role model. She was a godly person with great wisdom—Solomon had nothing on her. I loved to call her, just to get my daily: *"Let's all get up and dance to a song that was a hit before your mother was born, though she was born a long, long time ago, your mother should know."*

Why Your Mother Knows Best

No matter how many women you've encountered, you can't deny that your mom will always be the first(!) woman in your life, your number one and only one. There may be times when they'll have shortcomings, but time proves that mothers really know best.

Ten Reasons Why Mother Knows Best

We've all got one, the woman who's known you longer than anyone else, as if the two of you were separated at birth! She's always got your back because no one messes with her babies, and her love is unconditional. Moms always have a way of being right. No matter the situation, there are a few reasons why mother knows best.

1. She's known you longer than anyone else

She's the one who was there through the good, from your first words to graduating from high school. But she was also there changing your dirty diapers, and supporting you when you ignored her advice and did exactly what she told you not to. In her eyes no one knows you better and we've all gotten the "There's nothing on you I haven't seen before" line.

2. Every piece of advice she gives you is gold.

Sure, at the time it might come off as annoying. She's just worrying too much because she's a mom right? Wrong! As you get older you'll start to realize just how much your mom taught you. Every day I have to stop and say to myself "Wow, Mom was right!"

3. They always do their best to make you happy.

Nothing can replace the priceless moments, like when you have friends over and your mom tries to hang out to be "hip with the kids." As cringingly painful as that can be, there's a certain charm about your mom trying her best to be your friend. I wouldn't have it any other way.

4. There's no beating mom's home cooked meals

Even if your mom's not the best cook in the world, there's nothing like sitting down at the dinner table and enjoying a nice meal cooked with love. They might not be the best tacos in the world, but no one makes them like mom.

5. Honesty is the best policy when it comes to Mom.

Honesty is the most important thing in a successful relationship. If you give honesty you will receive honesty in return. Mom teaches honesty.

6. She loves you endlessly, no matter what the circumstances.

She has put an endless amount of time, love and effort into you, her baby, her joy, her light, and her life. She would go to any length to make sure you're happy, safe and okay, even if you make some mistakes along the way.

7. She is your #1 fan/supporter/cheerleader.

Ever since the day you were born, she has been your absolute biggest fan. Your first word, learning to walk, to read, to write, and to drive were all accomplishments treasured by her. Watching you graduate high school, college, or whatever path you follow she supports you and she cheers you on the whole way.

8. She always helps you understand and make the right choices.

Mom will talk you through the right choice, how to make that choice and help you understand why that choice is right. No matter the day or time. No matter if you have already talked about it over a thousand times before. She is always there to help.

9. The Golden Rule is the most important rule.

You get what you give. You must treat everyone the way that you wish to be treated. Mom always tells you that you don't know another person's life, so always be kind and treat others with the respect that you would wish to receive if the tables were turned.

10. Lastly, mom will never leave your side.
Through thick and thin, she will always be by your side, even if it is just you and her against the world. She loves you with all of her heart and being. She will do whatever it takes to make sure you succeed and will sacrifice whatever you need to keep you safe, happy and healthy.

Love to my momma. I thank her for all that she has done and sacrificed to give me the best life.

Admire Role Models, But Don't Worship Them

Sometimes people choose larger-than-life role models who are iconic and idolized by millions. Movie stars, professional athletes, and wealthy business moguls often capture the admiration of children and adults alike. In fact, sometimes people admire celebrities so much that their admiration verges on worship.

But they are human, just like the rest of us. They face many of the same types of struggles we face. They might not have to worry about where their next mortgage payment is coming from, but they still face criticism, competition, deception from people who want their money, and weariness from being in the public eye all the time.

> *John Lennon: "Why couldn't God make me Elvis?"*
> *Julia Lennon: " 'Cause he was saving you for John Lennon!"*
>
> *—Nowhere Boy*

Artist Chris Consani is known for creating iconic art that memorializes the 1940s and 50s. Many of his paintings depict Elvis Presley, Marilyn Monroe, James Dean, and Humphrey Bogart when they were in their prime—virile, lusty, cocky, and ready to take on the world!

Elvis Presley died prematurely, at age forty-two, after battling addiction to several types of drugs. James Dean expired in a car accident while driving under the influence at the age of twenty-four. Marilyn Monroe took her own life by overdosing on barbiturates at the age of thirty-six. Humphrey Bogart died at age fifty-seven as the result of cancer of the esophagus. Even while they were living well, they struggled with broken relationships, substance abuse, and other problems. Our heroes do not always reflect our deepest values.

Do you ever wonder what lies behind these icons' public images? What we see is their brilliance, talent, beauty, and incredible achievements, but do you ever wonder how they get along with their spouses or if they sleep peacefully at night? Do you ever wonder what it may cost them in terms of relationships with their children to achieve the pinnacle of "success"? Who do you idolize in the crevices of your mind? Are those well-known and wealthy individuals steeped in God's Word? Have they chosen the less-traveled path of humility, integrity, faithfulness, and commitment to the highest moral and spiritual standards?

What Is a Role Model?

My daughter wrote in her book, "Honest to Goodness Joy."

In my book, every day should be a day to celebrate Father's Day … I remember sneaking out really late (on a school night) for an epic concert. Here's the best part of the memory … it was with my dad. Some things never change as he will always be the coolest person I know and my favorite person to share music experiences and life with! Dad, I could never outgrow all the things I have loved doing with you. But, as I've gotten older, I've just learned to savor every moment even more. From concerts followed by Denny's to listening to old records to fashion shopping trips to cooking massive amounts of pasta to endless encouragement, laughter, and love. If I wrote out a detailed list of all the things I would want in a dad, my list would fall short of what God gave me. You have shown me love from the day I came into the world. You have protected and encouraged me and most of all—helped me become who I am today. I will always be your biggest fan and proud to be your daughter.

In 1991, I took my daughter, Daira, to The Eastern States Exposition, (The Big E), New England's great state fair covering six states, held in Springfield, Mass. As we walked down the midway, my daughter said, "Daddy, win me a prize." Daira was four years old at the time. Think of the pressure I was under! "Daddy's Little Girl," was asking her dad, her Hero, to win her a prize.

My wife looked at me like, "What are you going to do?"

Well, there was the ring toss on the bottles, darts, baseball pins knock down, basketball throw and "whack a mole," where the mole popped his head randomly out of a hole. That was it!!! You see, I was a drummer with fast hand/eye coordination.

"Let the games begin!" After five games at 100 percent victory, I was the winner. My cute, big blue-eyed daughter spotted her prize … a ten-inch bear, wearing sunglasses, a vest and a 70s outfit. As we left the park, with her in her stroller, she sang a made-up song about "The Big E Bear." She just told me she still has that bear. I never won anything before or after the monumental event. I didn't need to. Mission accomplished.

Role models are people who possess the qualities we would like to have and who affect us in a way that makes us want to be better people. They inspire us to advocate for ourselves, reach our goals, and take leadership on the issues we believe in. We often don't recognize our true role models until we have noticed our own personal growth and progress.

We encounter role models in every aspect of life. A role model is basically someone whose behavior is emulated by others. People are considered role models because of their success or the example they display in their values, beliefs, attitudes, and behaviors. Some role models are negative in that the behaviors that people emulate from them are not fully accepted, morally or socially. However, people should seek positive role models to follow and imitate.

A role model does not have to be the highest official in the land or the most acclaimed surgeon, actor, or writer. A role model can be just about anyone who inspires the desire to be just like them in a particular way. We all have goals and aspirations, and we look for someone who has accomplished or is accomplishing what we want to do, and we imitate that person. This imitation makes the person our role model.

Choose a Role Model Who Challenges You to Grow

Most everyone has a role model in his or her life. It could be a parent, a friend, a teacher, or a sports hero. It could be the D.A.R.E. officer who works in your school. It could be someone you read about in a book.

A role model is hard to define because it can be different for everyone. Who your role model is depends as much on you as it does on the person you admire. Often, it is someone you would like to be like when you get older, or someone who does something you find hard to do. It might be somebody who performs outstanding volunteer work. It might be a community leader. Maybe the person is generous and kind. Maybe he or she performed an extraordinary feat or accomplishment. It might be someone in your neighborhood or someone in another country.

Typically, a role model is brave, smart, strong, kind, thoughtful, and fun, but no role model is perfect—unless your role model is Jesus Christ. Role models might be outstanding in only one or two areas. Or maybe your role model is someone who is far less than perfect but is working to improve himself or herself.

Sometimes, people's role models are their mentors. This makes sense because a mentor is someone who excels in a technical or life skill you desire and is teaching you what he or she knows about it. You can tell a lot about which direction your life is heading by looking at the people you've chosen to spend your time with and share your ideas with. Their values and priorities impact the way you think and act. You are who you hang with. As they say, birds of a feather flock together.

> **"You are the average of the five people you spend the most time with."**
> **—Jim Rohn**

I believe people have many role models in their lives. Each role model teaches us about ourselves. To me, a role model is someone who not only treats me as an equal but is honest, trustworthy and most of all open-minded, especially in today's society which doesn't seem to celebrate people's differences. A role model *dares* you—and himself or herself—to be different.

Lately, I have been privileged to have some very young role models. I have been influenced by the vitality and passion that young women have in making their lives and the lives of others better. There is so much we can learn from our youth, but unfortunately, we often forget that.

I believe people who are role models recognize their position, whether they like it or not. It is their behavior that people look up to. It is their leadership qualities that others want to see and model. It's the smile they give to others, the look they give. It's the way they make us feel special just because we are in their presence. If you are out in your community, people are looking at you and noticing what you do. All the good things you do reflect on yourself and your family. We are here to take care of one another, and if it means modeling healthy behavior, someone must do it. Go for it.

Father always told me, "You're not going to get anywhere in life until you prove it to yourself." I was lucky to have my mother to remind me of that every day. It seems that role models have changed over the generations. People used to say their role models were people they didn't know, such as movie stars and professional athletes. Now people tend to choose role models who are in some way or another involved in their lives. I think this is great, and it emphasizes one of my favorite sayings "It takes a village to raise a child." I think the ideal role model isn't just someone whom you look up to or is successful, but someone who has had to go through similar struggles and challenges as you have.

Although we are often drawn to people who are a lot like us in temperament, professional stature, and economic status, my advice is to hang out with people who have accomplished more than you have. You can learn a lot from them. It's not always *comfortable* to associate with people who are ahead of you in their growth, but it's always *possible*. Try to cultivate relationships with people who can help you grow. Approach someone you admire, and ask him or her to be your mentor. Don't think only in terms of what you can gain. Always bring something to the table yourself. You've got to make the relationship win for both parties, or it won't last.

Surround Your Children with Positive Role Models

Everyone needs role models, and the earlier we are exposed to them, the better. Children and teenagers benefit greatly from choosing to follow the paths of those who are successful in life. Unfortunately, some role models can influence children and teenagers to follow a life of drugs, crime, and other negative behaviors that can ruin a person's life. If a child is surrounded by people who fail and do nothing positive with their lives, he or she might feel as though there is nothing wrong with living life like theirs. Some children and teenagers can easily be persuaded to fail in life like those negative role models.

Parents who have succeeded in life and live moral lives are teaching their children, through their example, that choosing to live this way is ideal.

Children who are impressed by such a lifestyle may choose to live the same kind of life their parents live.

Athletes, movie stars, and rock and roll singers are not the only people who can influence your children. A schoolteacher, pastor, relative, or friend who has a successful life can influence your children to do something positive with their lives. Parents who are divorced or single expose their children to other people who could be a positive missing male or female influence in their lives. See if there is a Big Brother and Big Sister program in your town. Or let your children participate in Boy Scouts and Girl Scouts of America. Encourage them to join character-building activities in their schools and churches.

If you are a parent, the most important thing you can do is spend time with your children, whether it's going to a movie or fishing. Children benefit from spending time with both parents. If there is a child in your family, such as a niece or nephew, or maybe a neighbor child whose parent has died, offer to be there for that child and to serve as a role model, someone they could look up to. They will be more than grateful for it.

Be a Mentor to Someone Else

If you are in a position of leadership, you can provide immense value to people in your organization who look up to you by being a mentor. The sense of pride and accomplishment you will feel when you make a difference in someone's life far surpasses the time and effort you will spend as a mentor. According to an article in the *Harvard Business Review*, effective mentors put the *relationship* with the protégé before the *mentorship*. They have genuine relationships with mentees. The best mentors go beyond building a mentee's skills for a specific position; they also help shape their mentees' character, values, self-awareness, empathy, and capacity for respect (Roche 1979).

Here are some tips on how to be a positive role model:

- Be diplomatic, straightforward, sensitive, and respectful.

- Lead with dignity and compassion.

- Maintain your composure under pressure.

- Educate by example, not empty words.

- Exhibit unyielding faith in peaceful solutions.

- Refuse to give up the cause for nonviolence.

- Combine honesty with tact and grace.

- Don't end a friendship or relationship after the first argument.

- Transform conflict into open conversation.

- Don't walk out on a discussion or mediation simply because it is difficult.

- Have intentions that reflect everyone's best interest, not just your own.

- Approach people on their level without being condescending.

- Refuse to respond to threats with aggression or force.

- Insist on focusing and finding solutions.

- Respect the feelings of others when expressing your own.

- Stay in touch with your heart and soul.

- Learn something from every experience and remember the lessons.

- Share your knowledge for the benefit of all.

- Remember that you are part of the human community.

A young woman might look up to a stay-at-home mom as a role model because that's what she aspires to be. Another young woman might consider the president as her role model as she sets her goal of becoming a politician. A young man might see his father as his role model because he considers his father to be the kind of father he wants to be in the future. Others may emulate famous sportsmen, rappers, singers, actors, and others who are in the public eye as their role models. Still, there are those who aspire to be professionals, so they will imitate or follow the example of teachers, doctors, lawyers, judges, accountants, and those in similar fields. Anyone can be a role model if someone sees something worthy of emulating in what the person does.

Role models provide the incentive that people need to achieve their goals. They also provide patterns of behavior that can serve as guides and positive influences for the people who really want to be like them. Role models serve as encouragement to those who would otherwise see a goal as unreachable. In your quest for role models, seek someone who can positively impact your life. Also, because anyone can be a role model, live always with the conscious thought that someone might be looking up to you as a role model.

Be a Role Model to Someone Across the Globe

As technology shrinks the world, you can easily be a role model to people across the globe. Today, people in developing countries are crying out for the expertise you possess. But this is big-league stuff, so only those possessed of courage, vision, and determination need apply. You as a business or professional person have leverage to influence others.

There are leadership opportunities anywhere we see a specific place where we can make a difference. This has to do with timing. We recognize that we have God-given gifts to use in helping make a difference. This has to do with confidence. We want to step out and address a need; hunger pushes us. This has to do with our passion.

In other chapters, I have discussed the incredible value that adversity plays in our lives. It teaches us resilience, self-reliance, and patience. And you have some gifts that you probably never would have discovered if not for the trials you survived. Use those skills to enhance your personal position so that you are the "One 2 Beat"! Don't forget to use them to help others, too.

RICHARD BRANSON'S RULES FOR SUCCESS

Top 10 Drum Tips—How to Become the "One 2 Beat"

1. Keep It Simple

2. Give It a Try

3. Be a Leader

4. Don't Give Up

5. Delegate

6. Treat People Well

7. Shake Things Up

8. People Will Be Skeptical

9. Affect Lives Positively

10. Do Things Differently

Before we move on to Beat 13, let's review the strategies covered in this chapter:

1. Admire role models, but don't worship them.

2. Choose a role model who challenges you to grow.

3. Surround your children with positive role models.

4. Be a mentor to someone else.

5. Be a role model to someone across the globe.

THE BEAT GOES ON
Your Legacy

"Drums keep pounding a rhythm to my brain."

**— Sonny and Cher,
"The Beat Goes On"
(Lyrics)**

Beginning in the late 1960s and into the early 70s, people were talking about "finding themselves," meaning that they were searching for a way to become self-fulfilled. People are always on a quest to find happiness and feel good. However, self-development is different from self-fulfillment. Sure, much of the time, developing your skills will make you feel good, but that is a by-product, not the goal. Self-development is a higher calling; it is the development of our potential so that we can fulfill the purpose God created us for. How well we do at fulfilling our purpose will determine the quality of the legacy that follows us after we are gone. After we die, the beat goes on.

A huge difference exists between a legacy and an inheritance. Anyone can leave an inheritance. It is something of monetary value you leave *to* your family or other loved ones. And it fades. But a legacy is something you leave *in* your family and other loved ones. I'm a "Human Time Machine" with seven decades of experience and wisdom.

God encourages us to fix our eyes on the things that endure. Leaders cannot become committed to the temporary. Leaders need to pursue a vision that outlives them—a vision connected to eternity.

Your Children Are the Best Part of Your Legacy

No matter what you accomplish in life, and no matter how much money you make, nothing contributes to your legacy more than your children's opinions of you. Similarly, no matter how badly you screw everything else up, if your children are good people who respect and love you, you have won. Your children are the best and most important part of your legacy.

I am blessed to have a phenomenal relationship with my children. Here is a note my daughter wrote about me one time:

> The man you see here is no ordinary man. He isn't the guy you meet and then ever forget you met him because he is rather unforgettable! He's passionate, enthusiastic, creative, talented, brave, determined, loving, and the best dad a daughter could ask for!

That means everything to me. Her and my Son are the most important part of my legacy.

Your Life Lessons Are Part of Your Legacy

The hard-earned lessons we learn throughout life's journey become a part of who we are. And the extent to which we learn from our mistakes becomes part of our legacy.

- Purpose sometimes changes, but passion shouldn't.

- A home-cooked Italian meal says "amore" (and more is the key!).

- You're never too young or too old to embark on a new dream.

- Never settle or live complacently.

- Don't be too hard on yourself—mistakes are free ways to learn!

- Displaying good manners will never go out of style.

- Tomorrow is only a day away, but today is a present, so don't pass up the surprise it holds.

- Everyone has a good side.

- To take on big challenges, you need tough skin but a tender heart.

- Age is just a number, and I'm choosing to stay twenty-nine years and twelve months!

> **"Life is 10 percent what happens to you and 90 percent how you react to it."**
> **—Irving Berlin**

What life lessons have shaped your view of life and the world? What improvements have you made to yourself after surviving hardships? What is your legacy? What will people say at your funeral? How much did you contribute to the growth and happiness of other people? We are given a limited amount of time, so we must use it wisely. Rid your life of BS. You get to design your agenda, but make it count for the long term.

> **"You can have everything in life you want if you will just help other people get what they want."**
> **—Zig Ziglar**

My Life Blessings

One New Year's Eve, as everyone else was downing the eggnog and watching the ball drop, I sat down and wrote a list of thirty things I had found to be true in the previous year. Here is my list:

- God's grace and love are far deeper than I'll ever truly understand.

- Finding a spouse who supports and cherishes you is an endless treasure chest of gold.

- Success is always worth celebrating, but failure often teaches you so much more.

- Humility and confidence are the most complimentary things you can put on.

- Identity in any singular thing (other than God) will eventually crumble.

- Joy is a choice, and God is the source.

- Mentoring someone leaves a forever imprint on your heart.

- All women are royalty.

- Traveling makes you a wonderful storyteller.

- Creativity allows your life to sparkle a little more brightly.

- God's wonder is all around—in every changing season and in every person you pass by.

- Change is not only necessary but a wonderful way to challenge, to grow, to regroup, and to push yourself forward.

- Strangers don't have to be …

- Being your own person means you don't compare your life with others' lives.

- Music is a forever "happy place."

- Loving yourself allows you to really love others.

- The best way to lead is to be the kind of person who is inspiring enough to follow.

- It is important to know your strengths and to be strong enough to operate in them.

- You must know your weaknesses and be strong enough to improve them.

- Family and friends shape you, but only God defines you.

A true legacy is more than leaving a large amount of money as an inheritance. Anyone can leave an inheritance of material value. An inheritance of money and things is something you leave to your family, or your loved ones, but it eventually fades. There is also an intangible legacy which can be passed on the family and friends. These are the differences between the two:

Inheritance:

1. something you give to others

2. temporarily brings some happiness

3. eventually fades as it is spent or wasted

4. your activity may or may not pay off.

Legacy:

1. something you place in others

2. permanently transforms them.

3. lives on long after you die

4. your activity becomes achievement.

Timelessness seems to embrace some and defy others

As so it seems to be true for us all; We are born, we live for a while, and we die. As Echo's, that guild those we leave behind, who themselves inherit their own echoes. And so on and so on—whose echoes can be as loud as thunder or quiet as a mouse there is greatness in them all.

If I were to wish for anything, I should not wish for wealth and power, but for the passionate sense of the potential, for the eye, which, ever young and ardent, sees the possible. Pleasure disappoints, possibility, never. And what wine is so sparkling, what so fragrant, what so intoxicating as possibility!

—Søren Kierkegaard

NAPOLEAN HILL'S RULES FOR SUCCESS

Top 10 Drum Tips—How to Become the "One 2 Beat"

1. Get Along Peacefully with Others

2. Believe

3. Have a Definite Purpose

4. Your Only Limit Is Yourself

5. Take Action

6. Improve Your Personality

7. Create, Recognize, and Act Upon Opportunities

8. Success Must Be Planned

9. Move with Courage and Determination

10. Conceive, Believe, Achieve

Before we move on to Beat 14, let's review the strategies we learned in this chapter:

1. Take actions now that will contribute to the legacy you leave after you are gone.

2. Nurture your relationships with your children and others. Contribute to their growth and happiness as much as you can.

3. Write down the life lessons that have impacted you the most. Also list the difficulties that have shaped your character and helped you grow.

RHYTHM OF LIFE
Living a Life of Significance

"Bobby, your story is still being written! Don't let anyone define you by a chapter— God completes the script!"

—Pastor Paula White-Cain

One day at Bible study, the speaker was giving an analogy of how God peels back the layer of our skin like peeling an onion to reveal our true selves. I raised my hand, and he said, "Ok, Mr. DelVecchio, do you have a comment to make?"

I said, "I think that's wrong, because peeling onions makes me cry. I see God peeling back our layers just like the leaves of an artichoke to get to the … heart. Man looks at the outward appearance, but God looks at the heart. While you are beautiful on the outside, I see your real beauty within your heart."

"That's very good, Mr. DelVecchio, can I borrow that?"

I read of a man who stood to speak
At the funeral of a friend.
He referred to the dates on the tombstone
From the beginning ... to the end.

He noted that first came the date of birth
And spoke the following date with tears,
But he said what mattered most of all
Was the dash between those years.

—Linda Ellis

I often meet people who want to do better in business. I ask them this question, "What do you want?"

Almost all of them tell me the same thing, "I want to be successful."

I can't tell you how many times I've responded, "If your goal is a life of significance, your work will be much more rewarding, pleasurable, and most likely, also successful, than if your goal is simply success."

Why is that? Because behind a facade of success, there is often a life of quiet desperation, anger, and unhappiness. This is because people think only of the outward appearance of success and not the inner feeling of importance and value in their own lives.

The saint, Mother Teresa, died at the age of eighty-seven with three garments to her name and a hundred dollars in her bank account. Yet around the world, millions recognize her name and her face and revere her for the work she did. Why? It was because she set out to live a life of meaning and significance, not simply a life of success.

Life Is Like a Piano

"Life is like a piano; the white keys represent happiness and the black show sadness. But as you go through life's journey, remember that the black keys also create music."

—Ehssan

In the late sixties, I was on tour with Dick Clark's "Caravan of Stars" and Richard Nader's "1950s Rock and Roll Revival." The cast of artists was: Chuck Berry, Little Richard, Bo Diddley, Chubby Checker, Jackie Wilson, The Coasters, The Drifters, The Dovells, Gary U.S. Bonds, and Bobby Comstock and Comstock LTD, of which I was the drummer. Imagine, a tour with all these black talented artists backed by skinny white boys … "Play that funky music, white boy!"

I remember the horror of prejudice in the South, as they were refused to eat in public restaurants and to use public restrooms. So much for being rock and roll "stars." It was like a scene out of the 2019 Academy Award Best picture of the year, *Green Book*. Today in 2020, prejudice still runs rampant in America.

The Beatles had previously taken a public stand on civil rights in 1964, when they refused to perform at a segregated concert at the Gator Bowl in Jacksonville, Florida. City officials relented, allowing the stadium to be integrated, and the band took to the stage.

"Ebony and ivory live together in perfect harmony"

—Paul McCartney / Stevie Wonder

The book, *100 Best Beatles Songs: A Passionate Fan's Guide*, tells us this about the song "Blackbird":

Blackbird" was inspired by media coverage of a civil rights rally, and when interpreted within that framework, the lyrics symbolically reflect the fight for freedom and personal rights. Also, when you consider the deeper meaning of the lyrics, the message stands out in stark contrast to the sunny, major key mojo of the song's music. Paul McCartney is encouraged, but he is also knowledgeable about that long, troubled history ("the dark black night") of the struggle for civil rights.

"Blackbird" is multi-dimensional and purposely ambivalent. Ponder the adjectives Paul uses: dead, broken, sunken, dark, and black. Grim, right? And then when combined with the choices of nouns, optimism "flies out of the window," so to speak: dead of night, broken wings, sunken eyes, and dark black night.

The verbs, however, are more optimistic: Waiting, singing, and flight. And capping off the message are four of the most elevated words in the English language: light, life, arise, and free.... "Blackbird" is art at its most profound. It is encouraging and uplifting, reflective, and sober.

"You say you want a revolution"
—The Beatles

Black people were forced to sit at the back of the bus, away from the white people. They did not have the right to vote. "A Baptist minister by training, Dr. Martin Luther King, Jr. sought to raise the public consciousness of racism, to end racial discrimination and segregation in the United States ... In 1955, King became involved in his first major civil rights campaign in Montgomery, Alabama, where buses were racially segregated" ("Martin").

"In his iconic speech at the Lincoln Memorial for the 1963 March on Washington for Jobs and Freedom, King urged America to "make real the promises of democracy." King synthesized portions of his earlier speeches to capture both the necessity for change and the potential for hope in American society" ("March").

> *"I have a dream that my four little children will one day live in a nation where they will not be judged by the color of their skin but by the content of their character."*
> **—Martin Luther King, Jr.**

Brave New World

> *"For the Times, They are A-changin'"*
> **—Bob Dylan**

As time fades, it is natural to look back to what we have accomplished and look ahead to what is possible. This is the time to take a profound assessment. We know what the future demands—a new approach to planning change. "Business as usual" is dead. To lead vibrant organizations into flourishing futures, consider an exercise that for generations has signified change: "spring cleaning." This practice is invaluable in the operations of today's organization and its leaders. Cleaning the attic, or "getting one's house in order," means first of all revisiting one's mission.

This short, powerful, and compelling statement of why the organization does what it does defines its reason for being. Powerful goals that reflect the organization's vision must flow from a passionate and relevant mission statement. From those goals flow objectives, action steps, and tactics that will carry the company forward.

I ask five classic questions: What is our mission? Who is our customer? What does the customer value? What are our results? What is our plan? The answers to these questions help build effective teams, deploy appropriate resources, and develop energetic businesses in response to goals and objectives.

An Idea Whose Time Has Come

There's nothing as powerful as an idea whose time has come. The time has come for a new infrastructure for wealth creation and for a new model of the organization. Timing in the business environment is everything. As a leader you can't possibly know enough or be in enough places to understand everything happening inside, and more importantly outside, your organization. But you *can* actively collect information that suggests new approaches. You can tap into a network of "listening posts" throughout the world. Knowledge gives you choices.

Look not just at how the pieces of your business model fit together, but at what doesn't fit. For instance, pay special attention to the marketing strategies of competitors, which are your best sources of information about operational weaknesses or unmet needs. Also search out broader signs of change, such as a competitor doing something different with successful results.

Creating New Strategic Methods

Many large businesses are changing quickly, others not so much. Sometimes change is driven not by company leaders but by the customers who rely on the organization for services. Yet despite early success, business leaders are in some ways naïve, believing that "if it isn't broken, why fix it?"

The answer, I believe, is simple: high growth organizations achieve so much, so quickly, because they create new strategic methods of marketing and selling their business concepts. Instead of imitating existing programs, these innovators take advantage of totally new methods that allow them to play games differently. What strong leaders seem to know is that no matter how actively methods are questioned, organizations inevitably fall back on old habits. Relative stability, satisfaction with past successes, even arrogance breed complacency. What is needed is not so much continuous improvement in marketing strategy (that should be a given), but periodic and unpredictable shocks to the recruiting system. However, it is one thing to get an early warning that trouble is brewing, and another thing to decide on a solution and then implement it. That is the real value of strong leadership: being able to see a different future and then having the courage to abandon the status quo and venture into new practices.

We need to continuously search for new strategies while we move forward in our current positions, strategies that challenge the basis of our existing business. Strategic innovation can only happen when we question our way of doing business and open our minds to new possibilities. Effective leaders have learned that to realize our business goals requires a road map, a business plan for the future. We must leave behind "business as usual."

Finding a Way Forward

My company, ZGroup Franchising, is a vertically integrated franchise sales and marketing company with a global reach that spans more than eighty countries. We maintain, support, and operate as a specialist in the franchise industry, aiming to position ourselves as a global force in territory marketing by providing franchisors with master franchisee candidates in all geographic markets.

Our management team has achieved a broad international network of high profile, key relationships throughout the world. Our focus is to capitalize on our network for possible marketing/sales efforts throughout the world. The launch this year of our new and innovative techniques for acquiring, qualifying, and closing master franchise and area development agreements will further distance us from the competition in advertising, marketing, and consulting services. The days of franchise advertising and recruiting programs using the "same old, same old" are over.

Focus on Giving

In my time as a businessperson and community member, I've met many people from all walks of life. Some have been blessed with money, good careers, and loving families, but they are very many unhappy people because they are preoccupied with getting more. The more you focus on what you don't have, the unhappier you will be.

Time and time again, the happiest people I know are not always the wealthiest. They are people who get satisfaction from being of service to the people around them. If you focus on what you can give instead of what you get, you will find that your life is much more worthwhile. Nothing has such a positive impact on a person as giving to others. To me, giving is the highest level of living.

I want you to learn how to drum up business and make more money, but at the end of the day, you are who you are. In other words, if you start off as a jerk and you make a lot of money, you're just going to be a bigger jerk. If you start off with humility and a big heart and you are kind to people, and then you make a lot of money, hopefully, you're going to maintain that same character after you experience wealth. You are who you are. In the end, it isn't about the money.

"It's not about money, not about fame. You are what you are. That's the name of the game."

—Dan Hartman

Remember that joy is not dependent on your circumstances. Some of the world's most miserable people are those whose circumstances seem the best. People who reach the top of the ladder of success are often surprised to find emptiness awaiting them.

Embrace the Old and the New

I drove by a construction site the other day and noticed almost twenty tractors demolishing a perfectly good building in order to build a completely new one. It seemed like such a waste of time, money, and resources. Just think of what could be done with that money to improve the lives of the homeless, veterans, single and struggling parents, and charities caring for the sick and needy.

I look at the small businesses that are going out of business and the big-box businesses like Circuit City and Kmart that went bankrupt. I think, *"What is going on with this world? Is the American Dream becoming the American Nightmare?"* People don't know what to do with their lives. They don't know how to make good choices. They seem to have lost all hope and faith in humanity. It's no surprise, then, that so many people have adopted that famous old *Gone with the Wind* quote, "Frankly, my dear, I don't give a damn," as their mantra in life. It's hard to care when people around you seem so immoral and disrespectful.

Here in the United States, the breakdown of community has led to increased levels of loneliness and alienation, which in turn create higher rates of depression, addiction, anxiety, and violence. We have to take the world back. We do not have to choose between the good ol' days and the new days. We can have both. Old can have a positive spin, as in time-ordered, time-tested, and time-proven. It doesn't always mean obsolete, archaic, or worn out. "Old" can suggest paths that are well traveled, truths that have stood the test of time, and customs and traditions that are familiar, meaningful, and dependable.

"New" has the connotation of something fresh, exhilarating, and invigorating. "New" means supple and vibrant. New things have the potential for growth. We can have the best of both worlds if we help other people get what they want. The reason you are here is important. God has a blueprint for your life that perfectly coincides with His eternal purpose, plan, and glory. No one else can or should do what He has ordained for you. Do your best to give peace, comfort, and hope to people. The goal is to find a good quality of life and a happy balance among work, friends, and family.

> *"The grass is always greener on the other side—until you get there and see it's AstroTurf. Symbols are never reality. Someone might have amassed material success and fame, but that doesn't mean they're happy. So, don't go judging a person's life by the cover."*
> **—Karen Salmansohn**

Time to Demonstrate Power

When you enter into the world of successful entrepreneurs, the one thing that every investor wants to see is a demonstration of your idea's or invention's power. What can you do for people? How can it affect the marketplace? And, most of all, how can it make prosperity? When a person comes to this place, many in the business world call it the "tipping point." This is especially true in the kingdom of God. There is a point where you must demonstrate God's power.

Richard Gazowsky has said,

> This is the point where the kingdom of God is established in your life, your family's life, your community's life, and your country's life. The reason I used so many references was that when God operates, He affects everything that you touch, from the smallest thing to the largest. Everything is influenced by a true, genuine demonstration to be built upon me, when I say this is the true foundation of your future life. I now understand that my future life is built entirely upon faith, which is the "substance of things hoped for and the evidence of things that are not seen." So, let me say it again, today, at this time, as it is going to build your foundation for your great future!

Put Family First

A note from my daughter:

> I know a man, who is no ordinary man … He isn't the guy you meet and then ever forget you met him because he is rather unforgettable! He's passionate, enthusiastic, creative, talented, brave, determined, loving and he is the best Dad a Daughter could ask for.

> Here's a little story (even though there are a billion I could share). When I first started dating, like any good father, my dad was very overprotective. He finally agreed to allow me to go on my first date but not without first meeting the "boy." The "boy" showed up at our front door and there was my dad with his hand tucked up his sleeve and the absolute

craziest looking hook attached to where his hand should have been.

He made the "boy" shake his crowbar (that he had sticking out of his coat sleeve), and then said … "you hurt her, I'll beat up your father!" Of course, I was mortified. The truth is my father has always been the perfect combination of keeping me grounded and close (in a loving overprotective way) and allowing me to fly. For this, and for so many more reasons, I am proud to call him my dad– "the best father in the world!

Today, people don't spend much time together. Fathers don't know what is important in their children's lives. There is more infidelity, and divorce is at an all-time high. In groups sitting in restaurants waiting for their food, everyone is checking their phones instead of talking with one another. The foundation of every society, the family, is crumbling.

Once, I was visiting a businessman who was at home with his family after being away on a business trip for a long time. We noticed that his son was playing sandlot baseball without a baseball glove, so we promptly went out and purchased one but when we gave the glove to his son, we realized that the glove we had purchased was right-handed, but the boy was left-handed. As you can imagine, there was no close bond between the father and his son. Imagine a father not knowing whether his son was right- or left-handed. In the business world, this dad was respected and recognized as a "success," but at home, he was an absolute failure, having sacrificed his family for his career.

Rhythm Of Life

A note from my son on his wedding day:

Dad,

Ellen and I want to thank you for all your support and advice through the journey that has brought us up to this point, and for your future guidance as we grow our marriage.

You are an incredible role model for how a father should take care of his children. Through all the hard times growing up, you taught me that "All you need is love."

As I am older, I appreciate your willingness to share your gift of drumming with me; whether it was supporting me in concert band, encouraging in drumline with me, or joining me in watching DCI (Drum Corp International) events.

Drumming has allowed us to bond as father and son, but furthermore, drumming has taught me to be creative and disciplined. I will always be thankful that I had your support while practicing and for showing me there's nothing you can do that can't be done.

Love, Sean

If you want to spend quality time with your children, you have to put in quality time and a quantity of time. You have to show your children that you love and value them by the amount of time you spend with them, not the gifts you buy them.

One question to ask yourself is, "Am I pleased with the reality that someday my children are going to be just like me?"

One Christmas, when my son, Sean, was nine years old, I bought him a basketball hoop. It had to be assembled, so we went outside with our tools and proceeded to put it together. During our assembly, my cell phone must have rung a dozen times until I finally turned it off. I was tempted to answer it, even though it was Christmas. After all, I make a living on the phone dealing with clients, but I resisted the temptation, and Sean and I played basketball for hours. I know because, by the end, I was exhausted. Afterward, Sean said to me, "This was my favorite day, Dad."

I said, "Really? Why? Because it's Christmas?"

"No," he said.

I asked, "Because you got a basketball hoop?"

"No," he replied again.

"Then why?" I asked.

With a smile on his face, he said, "Because I know how important your phone calls are, yet I must be more important because you didn't even answer one call when you were with me."

It brings tears to my eyes when I recall how much it meant to him for me to give him my undivided attention. My boy's greatest gift was the time I spent with him that day.

> **"My father's last words were, 'So much wasted time.' This will be a daily reminder for me to share my gratitude with those I love as to never waste another minute ... thank you."**
> **—David Cassidy's note.**

The best thing you can do is be true to yourself, who you are. I have put so much of my life, so much of what I love, what I long for in others; it's all about people seeing their life in what I've done and said, and it becomes part of their life. I want to give people the strength and encouragement to carry on.

Slow Down

"There is no music in the rest, but there is the making of music in it. In our whole life-melody the music is broken off here and there by 'rests,' and we foolishly think we have come to the end of the tune. God sends a time of forced leisure, sickness, disappointed plans, frustrated efforts, and makes a sudden pause in the choral hymn of our lives, and we lament that our voices must be silent, and our part missing in the music which ever goes to the ear of the Creator.

"How does the musician read the rest? See him beat the time with unvarying count, and catch up the next note true and steady, as if no breaking place had come between."

—John Ruskin

Once there was a man who was feverishly chopping wood. He noticed that his neighbor was chopping wood just as quickly. Then minutes later, the first man noticed that the second man was taking time to rest. When he saw that, he started to chop faster, and soon his neighbor was back chopping wood beside him. The first man chopped harder and faster, noticing that his neighbor would take frequent breaks. When he finally finished, he looked over at his neighbor's pile of wood and saw that it was twice as high. In bewilderment, he asked his neighbor, "How can you have chopped more wood than me? Every time I looked over at you, you were resting."

His neighbor replied, "No, I wasn't. I was sharpening my blade."

Allow yourself some time to be lazy and unproductive. Rest isn't a luxury; it's a necessity. Once in a while, turn down the lights and the volume. Turn down the throttle and the invitations. Less really can be more. Create a quiet place in your home or at work where you can go to think, plan, and recall your best memories. Take time to think, to ponder, to wonder, and to play with children.

Create a quiet place in your home or at work ...

> *"The deepest secret is that life is not a process of discovery, but a process of creation.*
>
> *You are not discovering yourself, but creating yourself anew.*
>
> *Seek therefore, not to find out who you are, but seek to determine who you want to be."*
> **—Neale Donald Walsch**

The Age of the Gentleman

That semi-imaginary time when we treated ladies like ladies might be over, but it doesn't have to be. We just need to set up a few ground rules for being a modern-day Cary Grant or Paul Newman.

- Keep all negative social media activities to a minimum because it's just not classy.

- Hold doors open for everyone because that's just a nice thing that you do.

- Always text back or return calls promptly.

- Own and be able to sufficiently rock at least one suit, accessorizing with a pair of nice shoes or a classy watch.

- Master a good handshake.

- Do your best not to put others down in order to elevate yourself.

- Call your mother often.

- Know how to cook at least a few good meals, because there is nothing worse than guys who assume it's up to the woman to do all the cooking.

- Make good eye contact.

- Treat every woman with the same amount of respect and humanity that you would your mother, sister, or daughter.

- Be compassionate, and know that you are allowed to experience the full range of human emotion. A real gentleman knows that the best thing about him is his ability to be kind.

"Every day that you talk and act is telling the world who you are."
—Bobby DelVecchio

Key Differences Between Morals and Ethics

- Morals deal with what is "right or wrong."

- Ethics deal with what is "good or evil."

- Morals are general guidelines framed by society.

- Morals are dictated by society, culture, or religion,

- Ethics are chosen by a person to govern his or her own life.

- Morals are concerned with principles of right and wrong.

- Ethics stress right and wrong conduct.

- Morals may vary from society to society and culture to culture.

- Morals do not have any applicability to business, whereas ethics are widely applicable in the business world and are known as business ethics.

- Morals are expressed in the form of statements, but ethics are not expressed in the form of statements.

Improving Your Life

In the year 2000, I was the Vice President of Franchising for Dale Carnegie Training. My whole family from my great grandfather, grandfather, father, brother, wife, and daughter were Dale Carnegie Graduates. The valuable lessons we learned from the courses we took had a profound impact and influence on our lives.

Dale Carnegie authored several bestsellers, including *How to Win Friends and Influence People* and *How to Stop Worrying and Start Living*. Over fifty million copies of Mr. Carnegie's books have been printed and published in thirty-eight languages. These are the Golden Rules developed by Dale Carnegie. I believe that these rules from Dale Carnegie's golden books will change anyone's mind positively, just by attempting to implement them. When such a change happens, it will change life for them and hence the lives of everyone that comes in touch with them.

Principles from How to Win Friends and Influence People (1998):

- Become a friendlier person.

- Don't criticize, condemn, or complain.

- Give honest, sincere appreciation.

- Arouse in the other person an eager want.

- Become genuinely interested in other people.

- Smile.

- Remember that a person's name, to that person, is the sweetest and most important sound in any language.

- Be a good listener. Encourage others to talk about themselves.

- Talk in terms of other people's interests.

- Make the other person feel important, and do it sincerely.

- Win people to your way of thinking.

- The only way to get the best of an argument is to avoid it.

- Show respect for the other person's opinion. Never say, "you're wrong."

- If you are wrong, admit it quickly and emphatically.

- Begin in a friendly way.

- Get the other person saying, "yes, yes" immediately.

- Let the other person do a great deal of the talking.

- Try honestly to see things from the other person's point of view.

- Be sympathetic with the other person's ideas and desires.

- Appeal to the nobler motives.

- Dramatize your ideas.

- Throw down a challenge.

- Be a leader.

- Begin with praise and honest appreciation.

- Call attention to people's mistakes indirectly.

- Talk about your own mistakes before criticizing the other person.

- Ask questions instead of giving direct orders.

- Let the other person save face.

- Praise the slightest improvement, and praise every improvement. Be "hearty in your approbation and lavish in your praise."

- Give the other person a fine reputation to live up to.

- Use encouragement. Make the fault seem easy to correct.

- Make the other person happy about doing the thing you suggest.

Principles from How to Stop Worrying and Start Living (2004):

- Live in "day-tight compartments."

- How to face trouble:

  ○ Basic Techniques in Analyzing Worry

  ○ Get all the facts.

  ○ Weigh all the facts—then come to a decision.

  ○ Once a decision is reached, act!

  ○ Write out and answer the following questions:

    - What is the problem?

    - What are the causes of the problem?

- What are the possible solutions?

- What is the best possible solution?

- Break the Worry Habit Before It Breaks You

  ○ Keep Busy.

  ○ Don't fuss about trifles.

  ○ Use the law of averages to outlaw your worries.

  ○ Cooperate with the inevitable.

  ○ Decide just how much anxiety a thing may be worth, and refuse to give it more.

  ○ Don't worry about the past.

- Cultivate a Mental Attitude That Will Bring You Peace and Happiness

- Don't worry about insomnia.

- Fill your mind with thoughts of peace, courage, health, and hope.

- Never try to get even with your enemies.

- Expect ingratitude.

- Count your blessings, not your troubles.

- Do not imitate others.

- Try to profit from your losses.

- Create happiness for others.

- The Perfect Way to Conquer Worry

  ○ Pray.

- ° Don't worry about criticism.

- ° Remember that unjust criticism is often a disguised compliment.

- ° Do the very best you can.

- ° Analyze your own mistakes and criticize yourself.

- ° Prevent fatigue and worry and keep your energy and spirits high.

- ° Rest before you get tired.

- Learn to relax at your work.

- Protect your health and appearance by relaxing at home.

- Apply these four good working habits:

- Clear your desk of all papers except those relating to the immediate problem at hand.

- Do things in the order of their importance.

- When you face a problem, solve it then and there if you have the facts necessary to make a decision.

- Learn to organize, deputize, and supervise.

- Put enthusiasm into your work.

Run Your Business with Bible-Based Values

If we run our businesses with rules we pull out of nowhere, there will be no rhyme, reason, or rhythm to our actions, decisions, or outcomes. I believe that when you run your business according to Bible-based values, you are following God's plan and operating according to unwavering guidelines.

We will be in a place where we do not know what is happening, but God is cutting the cloth of our lives by a pattern that causes us to look to Him. Most people lead a treadmill life, a life in which they can predict almost everything that will come their way. We must be detached from outward things and attach inwardly to the Lord alone in order to see His wonders. It is through the most difficult trials that God often brings the sweetest discoveries.

> *"Even in tragedy, God through His Word offers hope for those who seek and believe. It starts with the promise of a better tomorrow, of life everlasting, of eternal peace. It's called faith, and it offers hope where none existed."*
> **—Zig Ziglar**

This is an ingredient in God's plan for dealing with us. We are to enter a secret chamber of isolation in prayer and faith that is very fruitful. At certain times and places, God will build a mysterious wall about us. He will take away all the supports we customarily lean upon and will remove our ordinary ways of doing things. Then God will open us up to something divine, completely new and unexpected, that cannot be understood by examining our previous and current circumstances.

Pandemic Good?

> *You've got to get on the "good foot."*
> **—James Brown**

I've been guilty of always having a positive attitude during difficult times. To me, there's always a silver lining.

"It is your attitude, not your aptitude, that determines your altitude."

—**Zig Ziglar**

I'm not diminishing the horrible effects from this Coronavirus. But as I see it, here are some of the positive things that have come out of this pandemic.

My Top 20:

1. Family all together with kids

2. Eating at home with family

3. Social distance, Zig Ziglar says three-foot bubble

4. Playing games, puzzles

5. Listening to more music

6. Conserving money

7. Being creative

8. Reading more

9. Relaxing more—smell the roses

10. Vegetable planting

11. Loving more

12. Watching movies together

13. Calling friends to check in

14. Discovering new recipes

15. Washing more often

16. Praying more often

17. Having faith

18. Trusting in God

19. Exercising

20. Keeping healthy

"You meant to hurt me, but God turned your evil into good ...
—Genesis 50:20 (NCV).

Here are some tips for running your business with Bible-based values:

- Be trustworthy.

- Have integrity.

- Be reliable and dependable; keep your promises.

- Value the individual. Practice the Golden Rule in decision making.

- Value people, not wealth, prestige, or ego.

- Have honest and truthful communication.

- Motivate others through praise, not criticism.

- Work hard, but rest. Take vacations and breaks. Give yourself time and space.

- Remember that everyone is accountable to authority, especially to a higher authority.

- Remember that leaders are servants who have attracted a following because of their passion, vision, integrity, and love for people.

- Be resourceful. Don't waste the resources you have been entrusted with. Always be of service to others.

"Let there be nothing that hinders you from doing what must be done—accept the things to which faith binds you."
—Marcus Aurelius, "Meditations" (2000 years ago)

GANDHI'S
RULES FOR SUCCESS

Top 10 Drum Tips—How to Become the "One 2 Beat"

1. Change yourself.

2. You are in control.

3. Forgive and let it go.

4. Without action, you aren't going anywhere.

5. Take care of this moment.

6. Everyone is human.

7. Persist.

8. See the good in people and help them.

9. Be congruent, be authentic.

10. Continue to grow and evolve.

Before we move on to Beat 15, let's review the strategies we learned in this chapter:

1. Strive for significance, not success.

2. Leave more than an inheritance.

3. Focus on giving.

4. Embrace the old and the new.

5. Put family first.

6. Slow down.

7. Run your business with Bible-based values.

BACKSTAGE
Influences

"In my life I've loved them all."
—The Beatles "In My Life" (Lyrics)

This section is devoted to the people who have made a difference in my life. Some have been with me since the day I was born, some came along as I was growing up, and others serendipitously came into my life after I became an adult. I am grateful for the ways in which each of these wonderful people have touched my life and shown me things I could not have learned on my own.

People Who Have Influenced Me

I have been blessed to have so many wonderful people in my life. I hate to say it, but there are some days when I take those people for granted. I know I shouldn't; it just happens. But at the end of the day, I know I can always count on them, no matter what.

"When we seek to discover the best in others, we somehow bring out the best in ourselves."

—William Arthur Ward

People who have inspired me are not necessarily philanthropists, entrepreneurs, brilliant writers, prominent leaders, athletes, or movie stars. I'm not as impressed with their achievements as I am influenced by their decisions that have had a tremendous impact on their own lives and on the lives of those around them.

There's no denying that certain relationships are more challenging than others, but through each one, we have an opportunity to grow and help others do the same. Every relationship teaches us something about loving, trusting, forgiving, setting boundaries, taking care of ourselves, and taking care of each other. From the people who love you, to the people who challenge you, to the people who support you in life, be sure to show your gratitude.

As we grow older, we change, either for the better or, unfortunately, for the worse. Either way, people around us play a huge factor in changing our character. One person can make a huge difference in your life, whereas ten people all together might never change you.

In society today, it would be quite hard to live without being influenced by someone or some type of experience. Life is full of positive influences, and you choose which ones you're going to use for better or worse. There are also negative influences. The way you react to an influence determines what kind of impact you receive from it.

Just as the growth of tropical fish is determined by the size of the aquarium they live in, we are affected by our environment. If your current circumstances do nothing to help you grow, you're going to have a hard time growing to reach your potential. That's why it is crucial that you create an environment of growth around you. That environment should look like this:

1. Others are ahead of you.

2. You are challenged.

3. Your focus is on your work.

4.   The atmosphere is affirming.

5.   You are out of your comfort zone.

6.   Others are growing.

7.   There is a willingness to change.

8.   Growth is modeled and expected.

—John Maxwell

> *"The deepest secret is that life is not a process of discovery, but a process of creation. You are not discovering yourself, but creating yourself anew. Seek therefore, not to find out who you are, but seek to determine who you want to be.*
> **—Neale Donald Walsh**

These are the people who have had the biggest impact and influence on my life:

My Love: Jesus

God is the center of my life, and Jesus is my CEO. He is the First and Last, the Beginning and the End! He is the Keeper of creation and the Creator of all! He is the Architect of the universe and the Manager of all times. He always was, He always is, and He always will be … unmoved, unchanged, undefeated, and never undone! There is no greater love than divine love.

> He will never leave me, never forsake me, never mislead me or never forget me. When I fall, He lifts me up. When I fail, He forgives. When I am weak, He is strong. When

I am lost, He is the way. When I am afraid, He is my courage. When I stumble, He steadies me. When I am hurt, He heals me. When I ambroken, He mends me. When I am blind, He leads me. When I am hungry, He feeds me. When I face trials, He is with me. When I face persecution, He shields me. When I face problems, He comforts me. When I face loss, He provides for me. He is God, and He is faithful. I am His, and He is mine!

—Author Unknown

If you're wondering why I feel so secure, understand this: God is in control, I am on His side, and that means all is well with my soul. Every day is a blessing. I love the Lord and thank Him for all that He does in my life. Yes, I do love Jesus. He is my source of existence and Savior. He keeps me functioning every day. Without Him, I would be nothing. Without Him, I am nothing.

What I learned from Jesus was to love everyone.
When both my mom and dad died, all our friends and relatives went to eat after each funeral. I made it conditional that no one was to cry or be sad. It was a party, a celebration, where everyone could talk about all the great stories and memories they remembered about my mom and dad. I wanted them to rejoice in the fact that my parents are in heaven with our Heavenly Father.

"A soldier once said, 'When I die, do not play taps at my grave. Instead, play reveille, the morning call, the summons to arise'" (Cowman and Reimann 1997).

My Mom, Gina DelVecchio-Handy

Mom was a woman of God. She loved when I prayed for her. I called her almost every day just to hear her voice and then get another "golden nugget" of wisdom from her. I saw how much she loved her children, grandchildren, and great-grandchildren.

One day I said to her, "If my Plan A doesn't work out, I have a Plan B."

She replied, "Why have a Plan B? Why not have two Plan As? One plan is the one that you want to work out, and the second plan is the better plan A." How profound! How positive! It's the most brilliant thing my mother ever said to me related to business.

When I find myself alone and wondering who I should turn to now that my mom is no longer here, I am reminded of a scripture from the Bible, Proverbs 22:6: "Train up a child in the way he should go: and when he is old, he will not depart from it." (King James Version) So today, I talk to her in prayer, and I'm led by the spirit of discernment that she instilled in me.

She was a mom, a friend, a mentor, and the love of my life. She is missed here on Earth, but her spirit will live in me for eternity. One day, I firmly believe that I will be reunited in heaven with her. Everyone knew what a great cook she was, from neighbors to our band members, friends, and relatives. I once asked her, after watching her make my favorite meatballs, "How come I put in all the same ingredients that you do, but they are not quite the same? Did I miss an ingredient?"

She said with a smile, "Just add a little more TLC."

My son, Sean, once told me, "Your meatballs are great, Dad, almost as good as Grandma's." It felt so good to hear that. I'll take second place to my mom's cooking any day.

I know that to overcome such a great loss in life, we must accept the situation and be determined to make the best of it. Worrying about what we have lost or what has been taken from us will not make things better but will only prevent us from improving what remains. My mother didn't live a life of *success* as the world defines it, but she lived a life of *significance*.

My selfish self wants her to still be here, but if I cast down my flesh, I know that the pain she suffered was more than she could bear. One of my favorite musicians, Eric Clapton, wrote a song after the tragic death of his four-year-old son called "Tears in Heaven." It says that beyond the door that separates life and death, there will be no more tears.

For myself and on behalf of my brother and my family, I want to thank my step-dad Walt, for the care and kindness he showed to my mom. He used to sing to her in the morning, always upbeat, always holding her hand like two teenagers in love—a love that anyone would be envious of. I saw the way they looked at each other, with stars in their eyes. If I could have picked anyone to love and be with my mom, Walter would have been my first and only choice, but Jesus beat me to the punch. He knew before I did who was the best choice for my mom's best friend, companion, and husband. He not only loved her unconditionally; he also loved my brother and me like his own sons. What a man, what a role model he has been for us. I admire his character and love for people—always giving.

I know that my mom touched many of your lives, and I can assure you that she loved each and every one of you. Be thankful that she was part of your life. I pray for all of my family and her friends that you will find comfort in knowing that she is in the arms of Jesus.

She will be missed here on Earth, but her spirit will live in us for eternity. One day, I firmly believe that we will all be united in heaven with Jesus. Yes, I am proud to say I was a Mama's Boy.

When my mom died, I wrote the following tribute to her:

My Eulogy to My Mother
November 3, 2013

I've had a hard time sleeping these last few nights. I keep waking up in the middle of the night, tears in my eyes, trying to cope with the new reality that my mother, whom all of us loved so much, has gone on to be with Jesus. Despite all the grief, the pain, and the infinite night, the Lord is close beside us to protect and comfort us. He gave me this Word: "Let not your hearts be troubled. Believe in God; believe also in me. In my Father's house are many rooms; If it were not so, would I have told you that I go to prepare a place for you? And if I go and prepare a place for you, I will come again and will take you to myself, that where I am you may be also" (John 14:1-4 ESV).

Now she is with her sister and brothers; my grandmother, Fanny; Deloris and John Aielio; and all the rest of her family and friends who went on before her. They say we all have an angel in heaven; my brother's and my angels were just replaced with our mom.

What I learned from my mother: Never have a Plan B; have a better Plan A+ as a backup.

My Dad, Philip DelVecchio

I took the best traits of my father. You would only have to see the look in his eyes and the smile on his face, which told you that you did something great. Seeing him like that made me feel like I owned the world. My father was a dreamer, but his enthusiasm and love of life are what motivated me to be persistent in reaching my goals. He made a lot of mistakes and wrong choices in his life. We all have, but for him, the possibilities in life always outweighed the risks of personal loss or rejection. He always taught me respect and one of the most valuable lessons in life: standing up for what you believe in. He used to say, "Don't let anybody tell you otherwise."

For the first time in my life, I'll celebrate Father's Day this year without my dad. It has been said that the loss of a parent is one of life's most traumatic events. I now know the devastating truth of that statement. I've been told that, in time, the hurt will fade, only to be replaced by positive memories that soothe the soul. Already, I can feel that happening.

Though he may never have said it out loud, I know that he was really proud of what we have become. We are who we are now because we had a father like him. I remember when we were young, our father found time to support us in our music, from band concerts to Drum Corps contests. I don't think he ever missed one of our practices or performances.

I remember one night after a band concert my brother, Gary, and I were jumped by a group of angry teenagers who were mad at us because their girlfriends liked our band. My father and his brother spent the entire night searching for them to avenge their attack on us.

The loss of my father has been painful yet also strangely reaffirming because it has made me ever more aware of the rewards of our wonderful life together. Perhaps the most consoling words came from one of my best friends, who has known me most of my life: "Think of the legacy he left you, a curiosity about life, a hunger for knowledge, a passion for everything you do, an example of a life whose riches owe little to money, and a sense that anything is possible. Those are all great gifts."

I am very proud of him. But what I most appreciate about Dad is that he enjoyed life. He lived life in the present, not regretting the past or anticipating the future. He did it his way and enjoyed doing it. My father poured vast amounts of love and energy into me during my most formative years. He was a compassionate and generous man. He was not a very strict father, but we feared and respected him anyway (it must have been all those gruesome war stories he told us about when he was in the Marine Corps). He was a tough man, never backing down. He gave us a feeling of security and protection.

What I learned from my father was how to stand up for myself.
After my father died, I wrote the following tribute to him:

My Eulogy to My Father
March 8, 2008

I will always remember my father's fondness when perhaps every other circumstance relating to him is forgotten. This remembrance, I hope, will induce you to give careful attention to the words I am now going to leave with you.

Billy Graham was once asked what the greatest surprise of his life was. His answer was, "The brevity of it." As my father neared death, my brother and I put our hands in his and prayed the prayer of salvation with him. I wanted him to know that we were with him on his final journey on Earth and that Jesus was waiting to take care of him from this point on. God's Word says He has given us eternal life in His Son, Jesus.

As Dad lay dying in a hospice bed, his last conscious words to me echoed my last words to him: "I love you." The words were spoken just days before his death, a beautiful and a complete ending to a remarkable relationship.

My dad chose life as he faced death. He chose the fulfillment of life for himself by returning to the Father. He chose life for us by freeing us from seeing him losing his physical abilities and from the need to care for him.

I believe that a relationship does not end at death but reaches its perfection. This is the hope that manifests in my spirit. These next days, weeks, months, and years will prove my hope to be true, for my relationship with Dad will grow more intimate in my reflection and recollection. Indeed, I have already come to experience a better understanding and appreciation of my dad and what it means to be a father. I can now say things in my heart that I was afraid to share with him when he was here.

I've had a hard time sleeping these last few nights. I keep waking up in the middle of the night, tears in my eyes, trying to believe the new reality. But despite all the grief, the pain, the infinite night … amazingly, inexplicably, the sun keeps coming up. I am reminded in Psalm 23:4 that "Even when I walk through the darkest valley, I will not be afraid, for the Lord is close beside me to protect and comfort me" (paraphrased).

In conclusion, for myself and on behalf of my brother and my family, I want to thank my Aunt Doris, Dad's sister, and my Uncle Donald for all the care and kindness they have shown to Dad. Let's just remember everything my father shared with us. And let's be happy that he has finally gone home to our Creator.

My Daughter, Daira DelVecchio

My daughter is "Daddy's girl." Since she was born, we have had a connection unlike any other father-daughter relationship. I remember singing lullabies to my daughter Daira when she was a baby: the Beatles' "And I Love Her," "Till There Was You," "Yellow Submarine." As they say, "The apple doesn't fall far from the tree." She is like me in so many ways: a musician, a dreamer, an entrepreneur, a lover of fashion, intelligent, creative, discerning, kindhearted, and a positive thinker. Nothing sums up our relationship more than the following note, which she gave me on her wedding day, January 4, 2008:

My Dad—My Soundman

Music: From working on music together (medleys like "Girls Just Wanna Have Fun"), to enjoying music together (The Beatles, Jackie Wilson, Edgar Winter, and Eric Carmen), you have truly shaped my music and me as a skilled musician.

Sacrifice: I said, "Can I have some money?" and you gave me what you had. Even the little things like always filling up my car with gas—these are just some examples. The truth is, the security you have provided throughout my life, especially during my high school years, has made me strong. You have always come through and been there for me as a provider, even in the difficult times.

Love: Friends you made welcome, all the boys you protected me from, all the pep talks about dreaming big and working hard, and all the times you prayed and comforted me, have shown me your love was unfailing.

Whether it's a "tough love," "love that brags or admires," "love that gives and protects," or "love that is constant," you are the greatest symbol of love, like my heavenly Father.

Fun times: "Moon Over My Hammy" at Denny's after a concert, Daffy's clothing store, and New York shopping—twenty-four-hour marathons. Big salads and pasta servings to feed a thousand, all the times you traveled and brought home all the porcelain dolls, Christmas time—the gifts, the lights, the nutcrackers, which we enjoy all year—these are a few of my favorite things.

"Soundman:" This one has a double meaning! You never missed a single performance when I was growing up. Even if you were out of the country, you made it to my performances and always made sure my sound was perfect. This is also true about my life. Everything with you is positive—never negative, strong— never weak. You are my rock and anchor in the truest sense … thanks for keeping me sound!

Wisdom: You showed me through your wisdom how to grow up on my own. You let me drink wine (at home), go out without strict curfews, and have enough freedom not to rebel. You called me all the time, even if it was just to make sure I was safe, and that showed me you cared. You taught me to enjoy life but did not spoil it.

You might say, "What an extraordinary father!" But I say, "What an extraordinary daughter!"

What I learned from my daughter is always have a positive attitude.

My Son, Sean DelVecchio

My son, Sean, is the epitome of a "model son." Everyone who meets him, including his coworkers, friends, and acquaintances, falls in love with his humility and great attitude. His respect for people is profound. He excels in sports, academics, and music.

He currently has his master's degree in Engineering from Purdue University. He maintained a 4.0 average while working a full-time job at Lockheed. I used to joke with him and say, "When I grow up, I want to be just like you." Seriously, I've learned so much from my son. I became a better person just by watching what he does. He is conservative with his money, but not cheap. He is very humble and never brags (I do that for him). He is a "man's man" yet is very sensitive to people's feelings. He's tough but never fights. He's intelligent but not a know-it-all.

When I got divorced and he and his sister came to live with me, we didn't have it easy financially. When he was just eight years old, he walked into my home office and gave me an inspirational poem. Here is the first verse:

Don't You Quit

When things go wrong, as they sometimes will,
When the road you're trudging seems all uphill,
When the funds are low and the debts are high,
And you want to smile, but you have to sigh,
When care is pressing you down a bit,
Rest, if you must, but don't you quit.

—John Greenleaf Whittier

This is an exceptionally inspiring poem, with an extremely powerful message that applies to anyone and everyone. It's all about perseverance, tenacity, determination, and willpower not to give up, especially when things are going wrong, and when you are seemingly swimming against the tide. This poem reminds us that there are seeds of success in every failure, and that's why we mustn't quit. I like this poem because it rekindles our self-confidence, which essentially enables us to believe in our ability to achieve the goals that may appear beyond any rationale, common reasoning, and normal logic. This self-confidence is particularly important in life because it empowers us to bring our dreams and vision to fruition.

What I learned from my son was how to be humble.

My Pastor, Paula White-Cain

I met Paula at her church, New Destiny Christian Center. My first visit there changed my life forever. From the pulpit, she came off the stage, came up to me, put her arms around me, and said, "I pray that this cancer leaves his body now—in the name of Jesus, and by His stripes, he is healed." She had no way of knowing that I had been diagnosed with throat cancer just weeks before. She continued to pray for me every day through five months of chemo and radiation treatments and thereafter as I saw her at church.

She sent me emails of encouragement. Here are some examples of the encouraging things she wrote:

- God has someone waiting to celebrate you.
- The battle is always indicative of breakthrough. Your breakthrough is coming. Trust God. He has you covered.
- Worship your way through it.
- Some people may have left or abandoned you, but know that the Lord your God will never leave or forsake you.
- Expect God to do the impossible for you.
- I pray for strength for you to press in and push through.

- There's sudden defeat over every enemy trying to oppose your purpose.

- The battle might be too big for you, but it's nothing for God.

- God has an appointed time for your victory.

- Don't quit now; you're entering the season suddenly.

- God will give you supernatural strength for every weak and weary place in your life.

- I pray for the peace of God over you. In the name of Jesus, let the calming comfort of the Holy Spirit surround you."

What kind of a chance do you think cancer had to stay in my body? I thank you, Paula, for sharing God's Word with me, from His mouth to your lips. I will respect and honor you for the rest of my life.

What I learned from my pastor was how to have unfailing faith.

My Muse, Asha Morales

I have worked with Asha for more than fifteen years. As a vice president of franchise development, she franchises companies and helps them expand their networks globally. For as long as I can remember, she has been on the "same page" as me more than anyone else I've known. She is one of the most creative people I've met. Together, we come up with the most unique and creative ideas that anyone has ever dreamed.

Asha is kind spirited, creative, honest, persistent, hard-working, intelligent, inquisitive, and a fast learner. She is the director of marketing for Drumming Up Business. She is also a yoga teacher and implements her "in the moment" approach off the mat and into the business world with Drumming Up Business.

Her background encompasses a broad range of film and video productions. She has helped produce multimedia marketing campaigns and corporate training videos for clients such as Subway, Duke Hospital,

Rollins College, the Major League Baseball Association, and Publix. She has also worked with Oscar-nominated documentaries on several short films and documentaries.

What I learned from my muse was how to release my creative juices.

My Brother, Gary DelVecchio

They say that blood is thicker than water. Being only a year and a half apart in age, my brother and I did almost everything together. In our early years, we played in the band and drum corps together. But we also have our differences: Gary had a talent for building and remodeling, and I had right- and left-handed screwdrivers. He was a jokester, and I was the serious one. I was a strategic planner, and he lived for the moment. I loved kids, and he loved women. He was guarded, and I was transparent. I loved music, and he loved movies. He played bass, and I played drums, but we both grew up in a loving home, cherished by our parents.

What I learned from Gary was how to be content.

My First Drum Instructor, Joe Wormworth

I first met Joe in the summer of '64, when I joined the Magnificent Yankees Drum and Bugle Corps. I was fifteen years old. What an incredible musician and human being. He taught me more about discipline, perseverance, perfection, and hard work than anyone else had in my previous years. He was compassionate and kind, but someone who drove students to the brink of perfection in his drum compositions. I had so much respect for him. He was probably the most influential drum teacher I've ever worked with.

His dedication and love for me continued beyond music and Drum Corps. When my father and mother passed away, he was there for me at both funerals. Although I don't see or talk to him much, when I do, it's just like it was yesterday. I will honor and respect him forever. That's the kind of impact he has made in my life.

What I learned from my drum instructor is practice makes perfect.

My Childhood Friend, Paul Sorbello

I've known Paul since childhood. We grew up in Rome, New York, and have been friends for more than sixty years. Paul and I have played in bands together, toured the world together, worked together, laughed, cried, and lived together. He is like a second brother to me. He would always say that I was his hero, but actually, he was mine. I never met a more caring, selfless, and generous person in my life. We have never had an argument and have always shown the ultimate respect for each other. Paul is one who would "take a bullet" for me. I've never had a better friend, and I am blessed by the unconditional love he has for me.

What I learned from my friend was how to be kind.

My Bandmate, Dave Snellbacher

Dave was an incredible guitarist with whom I had the pleasure of playing. Dave has a great heart and is a great father, husband, and friend. He currently works in hospitals singing and playing for the elderly. He entertains them, while bringing them peace and comfort. Dave and I never ever had one disagreement or argument. He is laid back yet very ambitious. Dave is a witty and funny guy. I have only fond memories of our times together.

What I learned from Dave is how to be patient.

My Drumming Inspiration, Frank Briggs

Frank is a drummer's drummer. Although, I'd like to think that I inspired him to be a drummer, now he inspires me. He has played with a major recording artist, written several bestselling drum books, has a drum school, and recorded one of the best Fusion-Rock CDs ever (China Ranch).

What I learned from my inspirer was that anything is possible.

My "Japanese Father," Sir Dr. NakaMats

I have known Dr. NakaMats for more than thirty years as my mentor, friend, and business associate. He calls me his "American son." We have traveled the world together. He accepted the title of Honorary Chairman of the Development Advisory Board that I put together for Kids Beating Cancer at the Florida Hospital for Children. He has motivated me in my life and has been an inspiration to me as well.

Dr. NakaMats graduated from the University of Tokyo and is a Doctor of Engineering, Law, Medicine, Science, and Humanities. The US Science Academic Society named him as one of the world's top five scientists in history. (The other four are Archimedes, Michael Faraday, Marie Curie, and Nikola Tesla.)

He has patented more than 3,500 inventions. They include sixteen licensed patents to IBM (floppy disc, hard disc, tape transport), as well as the synthesizer, Cinemascope, digital display, fuel cell, karaoke, and many others. President George W. Bush bestowed on Dr. NakaMats the Presidential Award and the United States Congress Lifetime Achievement Award.

Dr. NakaMats serves as a representative of Japan for the United Nations Earth Day, and he is a recipient of the Gandhi World Peace Award. He has lectured as a senior professor at many universities, including Saint Louis University, Washington University, the Chicago

School of Medicine, the University of Southern California, the University of Arizona, Stanford University, the University of Central Florida, the University of San Diego, the University of Pennsylvania, Columbia University, MIT, Harvard, and more. I booked him on shows such as *Lifestyles of the Rich and Famous*, *That's Incredible!*, *The Tonight Show Starring Johnny Carson*, *Late Show with David Letterman*, and *The Merv Griffin Show* and at NBC, CBS, ABC, CNN, BBC, and RAI in Italy.

Dr. NakaMats and I both beat cancer at the same time. We have kindred spirits and a mutual respect for each other. I am currently writing a book for him called *The Invention of Love*.

What I learned from Dr. NakaMats was how to be persistent.

People in My Life (I Loved Them All)

To all my relatives and friends …

"I want to thank you falettinme be mice elf agin."

A — Asha Morales, Alejandra Rojas, Alexie Fonseca, Ariana Speirs, Augie Lamonica, Aaron Pearce, Alessandro DelVecchio, Ashley Fahlstrom, Abygail Joy Float, Arlene, Amanda Harris, Amy Hanna, Amy McDonough, Ana Marie-Codrean, Angie Shilliday, Anthony Montalbano, Anthony Stango, Alexandra Caruso, Adrienne Alberty, Angelo Cianfrocco, Andy Muse, Arnie Silver, AnneMarie ThornNelsen, Abel Beyene, Anthony Corollo, Allison Jenks, Adrianne Christy, Al Wilkes, Alayna Alyna, Alexandra Goodman, Alice Wouda, Alison Hanson, Alyce Vondrak Bartolomeo, Amanda Douglas, Amanda McDonell, Amanda Tokos, Amy Adormo, Andrew Muse, April Bradley, Arnie Silver, Amy Beckler, Angela Olea, Ash Sharma, Ashley Keys, Arlene McGrew, AnneMarie ThorNelsen, Anton Mordasov, Anna Aviega, Alan Gorge

B — Ben Ang, Buddy Rich, Bobby Comstock JR, Buce Hensal, Bryn Bertrone, Brett Frank, Bill Corsio, Bass King Avery, Brian Pearson,

Bryan Dowd, Becky Pearce, Ben Crosbie, Billyjoe Rouse, Bobby Petrella, Brad Carlton, Bruce Bowen, Bruce Merrin, Brad Knight, Bo Diddley, Bruno Oberman, Barbara Shelnutt-Vocale, Brian O'Connor, Bobby Caldwell

C — Celina Manzi, Careen Merz, Cassandra Hill, Carolina Restrepo Garza, Cassie Merei, Caty Roberts, Cecilia Briggs, Charlie Wells, Chris Gorgone, Chris Sifton, Candice Christman, Carl Zwisler, Cindi Cash, Corbin Johnson, Craig Stuart, Crystal Crystal, Cashmere Hunt, Celina Manzi, Carrie Rose, Carm Aeillo, Cindy Watson, Chantal Snellbacher, Carl Canedy, Carol Hensal, Carolina Garza, Cheryl Anderson, Christine Gregory, Christopher Page, Claire gale Schwartz, Claudia Ferro, Corbin Johnson, Craig DeLongy, Craig Stuart Wilson, Caroline Moore, Chuck Berry, Carl Canedy, Caitlin Havener, Catie Hoffman, Chandra Garbarino, Carmen Barretta, Chubby Checker, Cindy Watson, Chris Conner

D — Daira DelVecchio-Traynor, David Welday, Dr. NakaMats, Don Clowers, David Cheim, Dennis Puleo, Doug Thaler, Dino Danelli, Dan Hartman, Diana Lossing, Dominic Demeiri, Don Kleila, Donna Boyer, Doug Moncrief, Duke Shanahan, Damon Nai, Denny Kurir, Dani Brown, David Denegre, David Cruz, Diana Connery, David Snellbacher, David Sunday, Debbie Dorsey Robold, Derek Muse, Diana Basch, Doug Wilson, Dani Brown, Dominick Demeiri, Debra Farah, Danny Pickering, Dennis Puleo, Dale Rock, Dani Feffer, Debbie Clark, Dario Stucci, David Clowers, David Jamo Jamarusty, David Johnson, Deanna Carolina, Debra Nader, Dede Dabley, Dee Lynch, Dick Bottoff, Dina Joseph, Dina Mixon, Don Clowers, Doug Shackleford, Drew Paras, Duke Shanahan, Doc Qutie, Dave Simpson, Dick Bottoff, Debra Farah, David John Ward, Denise Gillette, Debra Lewis

E — Ellen DelVecchio, Edgar Winter, Eva Garcia, Ed Washburn, Elizabeth Star, Ed Wool, Elizabeth Henin, Elisa Fernandez, Emily Randall, E. Lawrence Benson, Edith Wiseman, Elisha Moleski, Eric Frank, Eric Ringdahl, Erin Forrester

F — Frank Briggs, Fred Kriss, Flora Manzi-Pacheco, Fran Cosmo, Fabio Scocimara, Faizun Kamal, Fred Kriss, Fof Antoniou

G — Gina DelVecchio-Handy, Gary Driscoll, Gary Ohlson, Garry Hall, Gina DelVecchio-Jenks, Gino Scialdone, Greg Saxonis, George McNeilly, Gary Briggs, Gabriel Vaccaro, Gabriela Herrera, Gregory Gasparini, Greg Mohr, George Harrison, Geoff Smith

H — Heath Williams, Heather Rice, Helmut Ghele, Heather Fagan, Helene Brotman, Holly Ford, Heather Thorn

I — Ilene Lieber

J — Jesus Christ, Josephine Lamonica, Jon Maple, John Cook, Joe Blockno, Jane Halbritter, Janelle Chapman, Jeff Fenholt, Jeff Tarantino, Jennifer Calabrese, Jennifer Ramsey, Jenny Mena Silviano, Jerry Jones, Jessica Danielle, Jessica Londono, Jim Robinson, Jimmy Cothern, Joe Wormworth, Joey Melotti, Johanna Ward, Joy Ross, Jonathan Cain, Jerry Summers, John Wnuk, Julia da Silva, Justin Baker, Jeff Hawkins, John Aiello, Johnny Aiello, Joseph Mariani, Julie de Silva, Jim Veigle, Jeff Sorrentino, Jennifer Ryan, Jennifer Calderon, Jennifer Elizabeth, Jen Rae, Jen Whitfield, Jen AC, Jill Emilimg, Jennifer Calabrese, Joey Manzi, Jessica Harper, Jessica Hallgren Kendrick, James Anno, Jan Ramsay, Jane Halbritter, Janelle Chapman, Janessa Siegal, Jay Bruno, Jaquay Pearce, Jeff Fenholt, Jeanie Ashbaugh, Jennifer Raybon, Jimmy Kale, Joe Bouchard, Joe Whiting, Johanna Ward, John Fitzgerald, John Sorbello, Julie Whittemore, Jackie Wilson, John Lennon, Janice Charles, Joe DelVecchio, Joy Ross, Jerry Gross, Jessica Harper, Jerry Turco, Jane DelVecchio

K — Kaseey Hudson, Kindra Lovejoy, Khabchanh Syriphone, Karen Kalinoski, Kasie Lynne, Kate O'Connor Ionelli, Kathy Murray, Kathleen Hawkins, Kathy Nai, Katrina Evans, Katrine Sterling Shorb, Kerry Parker, Kim De Hart, Kevin McDonough, Kim Murphy-Thompson, Kimberly Morrel, Kris Gault-Lewis, Krista Heslin, Kystiana Kali, Karen Lazer, Kayla DeVoogel

L — Lisa Christman, Lauren Christman, Lynn Rose, Lana Reynolds, Lauren Keys, Laurie Lorenze, Lindsay Armstrong, Lechon Kirb, Loren Brown, Lourdes Alberty, Lisa Simmons, LaDawn Lynch, Lainy Snellbacher, Lynn Sunday, Louie Amo, Larry Daniello, Laura Zorzi,

Leigh Valentine, Liang Liang, Larry Crowder, Lana Larrivee, Leah Parsons, Little Richard, Lori Destefano, Larry Hoppen, Lisa Hoffman

M — Mark Frank, Monique DelVecchio-Manzi, Mario Manzi, Mandy Newman, Michael Crom, Margaret Guedes, Matt Calabrese, Michelle Jones, Michael Maple, Morgan Fess, Mark Nai, Mario Ticlea, Mark Handy, Michele van Gelder, Murray Vienneau, Mike Franklin, Mary Gardner, Mary Malmquist Essenger, Mike Ebinger, Michael Andrews, Manny Lozano, Mark Stevens, Marlana Yarrington, Michele Nichols, Monica Chavero, Mike Ciccarelli, Marissa Marie Falitico, Melody Garcia, Marius Van Der Riet, Mathew Randal, Mathew Snaelbacher, Maggie Walas, Mallorie Nai, Marco Guirola, Mariel Miller, Marissa Marie Carollo, Mark Doyle, Marty Frank, Megan McDonough, Mellanie Nai, Michael Andrew, Melonie Magruder, Michael Jon Maple, Michael Mudd, Michel Eberhardt, Michele Hudson, Michelle Nai, Mickey Lee Soule, Mike Rusnak, Mike Demeo, Mitch Bucci, Melody Garcia, Michelle Oath, Marial Miller, Maurice Petrello, Mike Ferlo

N — Nancy Tarrentino, Nick Neonakis, Nicole Wilbur, Nancy Dair Leggett, Neil Weiss, Nickolas Hildyard, Nina O'Diva, Nicolas Zaldivar

O — Olivia Bailey

P — Philip DelVecchio, Paula White-Cain, Paul Sorbello, Pete Neonakis, Paula Wyatt, Patrick Randhall, Patrick Elsner, Pete Dominici, Pete Nash, Peter Miller, Phil Rowland, Phyllis Pieri, Pierrette Favreau, Pino Miraglia, Pudgie Carro, Paul McCartney, Pamela Wisner

R — Richard Mitchell, Ray Reneri, Ronnie Dio, Ronnie Colangelo, Ronnie Burnett, Rick Montalbano, Rick Derringer, Renee Maple, Ritch Mitchell, Radonda Dobbins, Renee Day, Richard Cianfracco, Rick Bruno, Robert Hernandez, Ray Sykes, Rachael Navarro, Ruth Cabella, Ringo Starr, Rachael Knight, Ralph Kubitzki, Ramona Reiner, Ray Colado, Raychel Acosta, Rebecca Larkin, Red Boswell, Rhonda Rouse, Rick Bruno, Rick Morgin, Ricki Wilkins, Robert Sarzo, Rob Scribner, Ron Sacco, Ron Wray, Rosario Sorbello, Russell Battelene, Rusty Geay, Ryan Bittinger, Ryan Scotson, Ron Tutt, Rod Pixley, Rickey Nelson, Richard Nader, Rod Pixley

S — Sean DelVecchio, Sean Traynor, Sean Maple, Sale Frank, Steve Frank, Scott Nai, Shelley Lewis, Shelby Lovejoy, Shawn Paris, Scott Thompson, Shannon Tate, Sarah Henson, Sally Facinelli, Sandy Hutnick, Scott Swimmer, Shanda Street Anderson, Shelly Lewis, Stephanie Anson, Stephanie Irzyk, Steve Barrett, Suzanne Dobson, Sam Certo, Sandy Baba, Sean Shannon, Sandy Hutnick, Samantha Jenks, Sarah Snellbacher, Sally Facinelli, Sam Guiliano, Sam and Leah Parsons, Samantha Tudor, Scott Cramer, Scott Griffiths, Sean Krimmer, Seth Lederman, Shanna White, Sharon Clowers, Sahron Knox Dietrich, Shawn Paris, Sheba Shadrach, Sheila Holt, Scott Fitzgerald, Stephanie Crdozzo, Stephanie Micelli, Steve Belko, Susan Jarvis, Seth Letherman, Sherry Page

T — Tom Portesy, Tony Cee, Tom Butler, Tempe Frank, Todd Lamphere, Tommy Curiale, Tom Lupo, Tim Franklin, Tim Coons, Todd Boren, Tom Reich, Troy Gage, Theodora Uniken Venema, Teresa Aiello, Tammy Georgine, Ted Mowry, Tony Cee, Tonya Scott, Tracy Turco, Tommy (Mugs) Cain, Ted Bogert, Ted Torres Martin, Telanda Kelly Sidari, Theodora Uniken Venema, Tom Allen, Tyler Allen, Thomas Klinlger, Tim Church, Tim Connors, Tina Nai, Tina Hui, Tiss Morrell, Todd Hobin, Todd Long, Todd Weiss, Tony Miceli, Tony Winiger, Tracy Hagerman, Tricia Engle-Bethel, Trish Sorbello Merkle, Trista Sue Kragh, Tom Standsbury

V — Vicki Brisbee Vince Brunetti, Vince Cogliano, VJ William Cerulli, Val Bryan, Vito Fera, Vinnie Esposito

W — Walter Handy, Wray Lynch, Willfredo Torres, Warren Robold, Wade Williams, Will Miller, Wade Cummins, William LaSante

Z — Zoraya Jelke, Zak Zakaluk, Zaheeda Durak

There Are Drummers:

Dino Danelli (The Rascals—I named my son, Sean Robert DelVecchio's twin, who went to Heaven pre-birth, Dino Danelli DelVecchio), Frank Briggs, Augie Lamonica, Joe Wormworth (Magnificent Yankees), Ed Washburn (Magnificent Yankees), Ritch Mitchell (Magnificent Yankees), Keith Moon (The Who), John Bonham (Led Zepplin), Gary Driscoll

(Elf), Buddy Rich, Gene Krupa, Roger Taylor (Queen), Terri Bozzio, Deen Castronovo (Journey), Greyson Nekrutman, Tommy (Mugs) Cain.

There Are People:
Jesus, Mom, Dad, Sean DelVecchio., Ellen DelVecchio, Daira Traynor, Sean Traynor., Gary DelVecchio, Asha Morales.

There Are Things to Do:
Drumming, Speaking, Writing, Movies, Concerts

There Are Things to Eat:
Eggplant, Pasta Rigatoni, Pizza, Fish, Vegetables, Fruit

There Are Things to Drink:
Water, Almond Milk, Wine, Lemonade, Green Tea, Beer, Tequila, Vodka

There Are Places in My Life:
In the States: New York City; Dallas, Texas; Orlando, Florida; Newport, Rhode Island; Los Angeles, California; Las Vegas, Nevada; Rome, New York

Cities abroad: Rome, London, Paris, Tokyo, Lisbon, Sydney, Milan, Singapore, Hong Kong

Other countries: Colombia, Mexico, Japan, Italy, Singapore, Hong Kong, England

There Are Things in My Life:
New Destiny Christian Center, drumming, cooking, plays, concerts, movies, public speaking, writing, Kids Beating Cancer, Florida Hospital for Children, Camp Boggy Creek, The Rotary Club, Story Life Church

There Are Bands in My Life:
The Who, The Beatles, ELO, AC/DC, Led Zeppelin, Queen, Elves, Young Rascals, The Hollies, The Zombies, The Edgar Winter Group, Rick Derringer, Journey

There Are Songs in My Life:
"Gonna Have a Good Time Tonight," "Eleanor Rigby," "Friday on My Mind," "The Sun Ain't Gonna Shine," "Higher and Higher," "Blackbird," "Let It Be," "Hey Jude," "Good Loving," "Needles and Pins," "You Shook Me All Night Long," "Tin Soldier," "Frankenstein," "Rock and Roll Hoochie Coo."

There Are Movies in My Life:
My Cousin Vinnie, The Greatest Showman, Bohemian Rhapsody, Happy Feet, Ten Commandments, Rocketman, Yesterday, Wayne's World, Up in Smoke

There Are Books in My Life:
Bible, *Drumming Up Business*, *Wild at Heart*, *Halftime*, *How to Win Friends and Influence People*

There Are TV Shows in My Life:
Seinfeld, Shark Tank, The Voice, America's Got Talent, Grammys

When people think about you, do they say to themselves, "My life is better because of that person?" Their response probably answers the question of whether you are adding value to them. To succeed personally, you must try to help others. That's why Zig Ziglar says, "You can have everything in life you want, if you will just help other people get what they want." How do you do that? You turn your focus from yourself and start adding value to others.

First Things First

I met a young group of entrepreneurs at a Franchise Show in Boston. Knowing my background of victories and failures that I've had in my life, they asked me, "What do you believe is the reason for your accomplishments, and what tips can you give us, that will help us achieve success?"

I answered, "Are you ready for this?"

They said, "Yes!"

I stated, "Do you want to know the Truth?"

"Yes," they replied.

I commanded, "Can you handle the Truth?"

"YES, YES," they shouted!

"I have learned to put God first in my life!!!"

> *"I know the plans that the Lord has for me; to prosper me, not to harm me, and plans to give me hope and a future."*
> **—Jeremiah 29:11**

- God first in my Money

- God first in my Relationships

- God first in my Work

- God first in my Health

- God first in my Recreation

I can do all things through Christ who strengthens me."

—Phil. 4:13 (Evangelical Heritage Version)

"Because, if God is not the center of everything I do, say, or be, I'M NOT INTERESTED!!!"

"And in the End the Love You Take,
is Equal to the Love You Make"

When you've come "thus far" in your life's journey, you realize that you have not yet come to the end of the road and you still have some distance to travel. There are still more trials, joys, temptations, battles, defeats, victories, prayers, answers, toils, and strengths to come. "Be strong and take heart" (Ps. 27:14) and with thanksgiving and confidence, lift your voice and praise the Lord who "thus far" has helped you. This is your year of restoration, vindication and blessings. No matter what the future has in store for you.

"And someday in the mist of time
When they asked me if I knew you,
I'd smile and say you were a friend of mine ...
And the sadness would be lifted from my eyes;
Oh when I'm Old and Wise."

—Alan Parsons Project

MOTHER TERESA'S RULES FOR SUCCESS

Top 10 Drum Tips—How to Become the "One 2 Beat"

1. Love Them Anyway

2. Love Them Anyway

3. Succeed Anyway

4. Do Good Anyway

5. Be Honest and Frank Always

6. Think Anyway

7. Fight For a Few Underdogs Anyway

8. Build Anyway

9. Help People Anyway

10. Give Your World the Best You Have Anyway

DRUM ROLL PLEASE ...
About the Author—Music is my oxygen!

Bobby and the Beat

I want to tell you about a person I know named Bob. Bob knows how to create wins, and everyone who meets him witnesses his many successes, but this wasn't always the case. Bob grew up in poverty but also with a high expectation that he had everything he needed to have a rich life. He was a natural musician but without money to afford lessons, he began his training in a pretty unique way. His mother, a dancer, would spend countless hours in the studio where young Bob would listen to the feet of the tap dancers and mimic the sounds he heard with his hands.

After years of teaching himself the drums, he dropped out of school to become a full-time musician. While living on the road can be tough, he focused on his passion and found small wins in the most creative ways. He once told me that he felt he had experienced a great win because he got to play a show at a McDonalds opening and his payment was all the food that he could eat! He considered every time he got to do what he loved a win. He played every dive bar and smoky club you could imagine. If an owner would have his band play, he would be there. Thousands of shows later, every small win created this next big win: a coveted spot on a national tour, including playing at the first Woodstock.

Fast forward several gold albums and decades later and something happened where he could no longer consider life on the road a win. After this major turning point happened in his life, he set out to reinvent himself, without a college degree.

As a positive go-getter, he knew nothing could stop him from his next series of wins, and so he began to invest in inspirational books like those by Dale Carnegie (who he would later work for) and Zig Ziglar. He invested his time in becoming knowledgeable about how to make a sale, and he set small goals that he could accomplish.

His first goal as a door-to-door salesman was to train with the best. He would study those who were great at closing the deal and find ways to replicate what made them successful. Now, there is nothing glorious about hearing "no" hundreds of times a month during his training, but he knew that his determination would eventually create a win.

He would often remind himself that he wasn't losing but rather pre-winning. With a glass-half-full attitude, he began closing sales. Sale after sale helped in creating the momentum he needed not only to win but to build the confidence to become a great salesman. Fast forward yet again.

Years later, he was no longer selling one product door to door, but entire franchises for multi-million-dollar companies. Bob never stopped celebrating his wins, whether it was his humble beginnings that taught him to work hard, his good ole days in the band or his first major sale that led to millions. As he began to win, he saw himself as nothing less even when times were increasingly tough. He recalls trying to sell franchises after the tragedy of 9/11, when no one wanted to invest their money. Regardless of the challenges, he prevailed and created one small win at a time.

Now … I may be biased because Bob is actually my dad and the major change that made him no longer want a life on the road was having me, his daughter. But I can't help but think that some of my wins are because he taught me what it looked like first. We all need to be like

Bob and start small; every win can build momentum to our biggest wins that are yet to come!

Dad, the man who taught me how to dream and do! If you ask me, he's been pretty amazing! He doesn't know this yet, but in the book that I am writing on how to design a life you love, he's my very appropriate story/example on the chapter entitled "Wins." Dad, this one is for you!

—Daira DelVecchio-Traynor

The Center Stage

Being on stage moves us to another level, away from the boundaries that suggest limits and narrow perspectives, to a different sort of arena where we see new possibilities, where imagination and creative impulses flourish and are encouraged.
—The Edutainer: Brad Johnson, Tammy Maxson McElroy

Music has been a huge part of Bob DelVecchio's life. An innovative and creative thinker, Bob draws his inspiration from his previous career as a world-class drummer with Bobby Del and the Deltones, The Aftermath, Comstock LTD, Loch Ness, Dick Clark's "Caravan of Stars," Little Richard, Chuck Berry, Chubby Checker, Jackie Wilson, Bo Diddley, The Dovells, The Shirelles, The Coasters, The Drifters, The Five Satins, Gary U. S. Bonds, The Edgar Winter Group, and Rick Derringer. The impact and inspiration music has imparted extends to everything he has done, both personally and professionally.

The Beat Goes On

Bob served as the Senior Vice President of Franchise Development for Dale Carnegie Training and U2's Q-Zar Entertainment, where he negotiated the exclusive rights as game supplier to the 1996 Olympics. Currently Bob is the Founder/CEO of Z Group Franchising which represents the top franchises of their industries.

A Life of Significance

Bob is the founder and managing director of Drumming Up Business. His program "Beating the Odds" has expanded to working with kids beating cancer and other debilitating diseases all over the world. In the US, The Great American Franchise Expo sponsors the "Beating the Odds" foundation by giving 100 percent of ticket sales. Bob has found a life that really matters, one that has taken him from success to significance.

Entertainment and entrepreneurship have instilled in Bob many lifelong skills that give Bob a passion to motivate, inspire, teach, and lead; and eventually become one of the most captivating speakers in the world today.

A good friend and partner of Bob's, Asha Morales said, "You're one of the best storytellers ever," to which he responded, "That's funny, the smartest living human being in the entire world, Sir Dr. NakaMats said the same thing. You guys are on the same level, you're both geniuses. I think I just missed my flight!"

"And now you know the rest of the story."
—Paul Harvey

BOB DELVECCHIO'S RULES FOR SUCCESS

Top 10 Drum Tips—How to Become the "One 2 Beat"

1. God Is the Center of Life

2. Become a "Roll Model"

3. Have a Compelling Purpose

4. Commit to a Cause

5. Dream B.I.G. (Believing in God)

6. March to the Beat of Your Own Drum

7. Have a HeartBEAT to Serve

8. Have a "Good Foot" Attitude

9. Never Surrender

10. Make a Ton of Money—Have a Ton of Fun

RUDIMENTS
REFERENCES

Adhvaryu, Achyuta. "Soft Skills Training Boosts Productivity." *Michigan News.* January 19, 2017. https://news. umich.edu/soft-skills-training-boosts-productivity/.

"Michelangelo Biography." *Biography.com.* Last updated March 4, 2020. https://www.biography.com/artist/michelangelo.

Bruce, Jan. "Why Soft Skills Matter And The Top 3 You Need." *Forbes.* March 10, 2017. https://www.forbes.com/ sites/janbruce/2017/03/10/why-soft-skills-matter-and-the-top-3-you-need/?sh=629fcbc076f3.

Campbell, Don. *The Mozart Effect: Tapping the Power of Music to Heal the Body, Strengthen the Mind, and Unlock the Creative Spirit.* New York: Quill, 2001.

Carnegie, Dale. *How to Win Friends & Influence People.* New York: Pocket Books, 1998.

Carnegie, Dale. *How to Stop Worrying and Start Living.* New York: Gallery Books, 2004.

Cleland, Gary. "Drummers Are Natural Intellectuals." *The Telegraph*, April 17, 2008. https://www.telegraph.co.uk/news/uknews/1895839/Drummers-are-natural-intellectuals.html.

Cowman, L. B. E. and Jim Reimann. *Streams in the Desert: 366 Daily Devotional Readings.* New York: Zondervan, 2001.

Cowman, L. B. E. *Streams in the Desert Morning and Evening: 365 Devotions.* New York: Zondervan, 2016.

Dholakia, Utpal. "How Terrorist Attacks Influence Consumer Behaviors: The Adverse Effects of Behavior Shifts on Business & the Environment." *Psychology Today*, December 1, 2015. https://www.psychologytoday.com/us/ blog/the-science-behind-behavior/201512/how-terrorist-attacks-influence-consumer-behaviors.

Gonzales, Bryan. "Sales Development Technology: The Stack Emerges." *Topo-Blog*, accessed December 17, 2020. http://blog.topohq.com/sales-development-technology-the-stack-emerges/.

Greenspan, Jesse. "10 Things You May Not Know About Churchill." *History.com*, April 9, 2014. http://www.history.com/news/10-things-you-may-not-know-about-winston-churchill.

"HeartRhythms – Benefits of Participation." *Remo*. https://remo. com/experi-ence/post/healthrhythms-benefits- of-participation/.

Hill, Dwight. "The Battle Within." *Net Profits*, January 9, 1995. http://www.antioch.com.sg/well/devotional/ dwight/94/94-01-09.htm.

Jacobs, Tom. "Musical Meds." *Pacific Standard,* June 14, 2017. https://psmag.com/economics/drummers-high-evidence-that-playing-music-releases-endor-phins-49578.

Lang, Rusty A. *Good Things Take Time: Metamorphosis of a Damaged Soul.* Book-locker.com, Inc.,2018.

Lewis, Michael, and Stephen J. Spignesi. *100 Best Beatles Songs: A Passionate Fan's Guide.* New York: Running Press, 2009.

"Life's Trials." *The Barry Agency.* http://www.thebarryagency.com/ Christian/ Womens%20Ministries%20Articles/2009_ Feb_Newsletter.htm

Madden, Blake. "The Resonant Human: The Science of How Tempo Affects Us." *SonicScoop,* June 19, 2014. https://sonicscoop.com/2014/06/19/the-reso-nant-human-the-science-of-how-tempo-affects-us/.

"March on Washington for Jobs and Freedom, 1963." *Stanford: The Martin Luther King, Jr. Research and Education Institute*, accessed December 16, 2020. https://kinginstitute.stanford.edu/mlk-topic/march-washington-jobs-and- free-dom-1963?page=2.

"Martin Luther King, Jr: Fighting for Equal Rights in America." *Tolerance Project,* accessed December 16, 2020. https:// tolerance.tavaana.org/en/content/martin-luther-king-jr-fighting-equal-rights-america.

Otar, Chad. "What Percentage of Small Businesses Fail—And How Can You Avoid Being One of Them?" *Forbes*, October 25, 2018. https://www.forbes.com/sites/forbes-financecouncil/2018/10/25/what-percentage-of-small- businesses-fail-and-how-can-you-avoid-being-one-of-them/?sh=3686c2e143b5.

Otberg, John. *If You Want to Walk on Water, You've Got to Get Out of the Boat.* New York: Zondervan, 2001

Peeples, Lynne. "Heat Beat: Music May Help Keep Your Cardiovascular System in Tune." *Scientific American*, June 24, 2009. https://www.scientificamerican.com/article/ music-therapy-heart-cardiovascular/.

Ramus, Franck. "Language Discrimination by Newborns: Teasing Apart Phonotactic, Rhythmic, and Intonational Cues." *Annual Review of Language*, October 1, 2002. https://doi.org/10.1075/arla.2.05ram.

Roche, Gerald R. "Much Ado About Mentors." *Harvard Business Review*, January 1979. https://hbr.org/1979/01/ much-ado-about-mentors.

Shan, Jiang. 2014. "Baroque Music Makes Us Smarter?" *SiOW- fa14 Science in Our World: Certainty and Cont*, December 5, 2014. https://sites.psu.edu/siow-fa14/2014/12/05/baroque-music-makes-us-smarter/.

Singer, Emily. "Molecular Basis for Mozart Effect Revealed." *NewScientist*, April 23, 2004. https://www.newscientist.com/article/dn4918-molecular-basis-for-mozart-effect-revealed/.

Sitkin, S.B. "Learning through Failure: The Strategy of Small Losses." *Research in Organizational Behavior*, 14 (1992): 231-266.

Society of Rock. "Listening to AC/DC Can Help You Fight Cancer, Study Says—But Not For the Reason You're Thinking." accessed December 16, 2020. https://societyofrock.com/ listening-to-ac-dc-can-help-you-fight-cancer-study-says- but-not-for-the-reason-you're-thinking/.

Young, Sarah. *Jesus Today: Experience Hope Through His Presence*. Nashville: Thomas Nelson, 2012.

INTRODUCING...
My Daughter Daira

Let me introduce you to my Daughter Daira. When she was a baby, I would see her in her crib smiling—what a positive child. It's no wonder that in her adult years she would write a book entitled "Honest to Goodness Joy." Check it out if you want more Joy in your life...It'll make you smile.

Joy Has a Name On It!

What if you didn't have to wait for a vacation, promotion, or winning lottery ticket to experience, authentic Joy?

What if you believe that Joy was available to you every day?

Maybe you are shutting the world out because you're facing anxiety. No one knows about.

Baby, you are chasing the next high, because you're wrestling with depression.

Maybe you are working long hours because you're feeling empty inside.

Maybe you thought you were happy until life unexpectedly came crashing down.

Honest to goodness. Joy was written with you in mine.

Do you think Joy is only for a select few in you'll never be invited to the party?

Good news is that based on who you are.

You could be confident in who God made you to be.

You can take risk and bravely face your fears.

You can experience wins and celebrate the little things that become the big things. You can survive a tragedy and hope and find hope that you never thought possible.

This book will challenge you to fight for a life marked by Joy and practice it daily.

Are you ready to stop claiming depression, anxiety, in difference, or complacency, and replace them with a joy that overflows?

By: Daira Avery Traynor

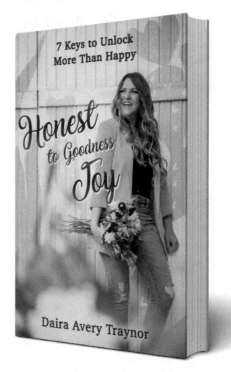

"YOUR BEST MUSIC HAS YET TO BE PLAYED"

If you enjoyed this book...

There are several ways you can help get the message out:

- Post a 5-star review on Amazon.
- Write about the book on your Facebook, Twitter, Instagram, LinkedIn, etc.
- If you blog, consider referencing the book or publishing an excerpt from the book.
- You have my permission to do this. Please provide proper credits.
- Recommend the book to friends—word of mouth is the most effective advertising.
- Purchase additional copies to give away as gifts.

Learn more by visiting BobbyDelVecchio.com.

Need a Dynamic Speaker for Your Next Event?

A "Rocking Revolution"

In Drumming Up Business seminars, music is our foundation. It has been formulated to provide an environment where the participants are engaged, encouraged, inspired and challenged.

Drumming can dramatically improve physiological, mental, and physical coordination which makes it an extremely effective catalyst for learning and development.

These action packed seminars are a dynamic mixture of drumming, showmanship, training and education (Edutainment). We will keep the audience alive and inspired; while they receive a wealth of knowledge and information. These seminars range from one-hour to three-hour sessions, to a three-day workshop that can be tailored to the audience's needs. AND YES...You will Be Drumming.

Learn more by visiting: DrummingUpBusiness.com
Or email: Bobby@drummingupbusiness.com